DATE DUE

DEMCO 38-296

Working With
CHALLENGING
PARENTS
of Students
With
Special Needs

To David

Working With
CHALLENGING
PARENTS
of Students
With
Special Needs

JEAN CHENG GORMAN

CORWIN PRESS
A Sage Publications Company
Thousand Oaks, California

For information:

Corwin Press
A Sage Publications Company
2455 Teller Road
Thousand Oaks, California 91320
www.corwinpress.com

Sage Publications Ltd.
1 Oliver's Yard
55 City Road
London EC1Y 1SP
United Kingdom

Sage Publications India Pvt. Ltd.
B-42, Panchsheel Enclave
Post Box 4109
New Delhi 110 017 India

Printed in the United States of America

Library of Congress Cataloging-in-Publication Data

Gorman, Jean Cheng.
Working with challenging parents of students with special needs / Jean Cheng Gorman.
   p. cm.
Includes bibliographical references and index.
ISBN 0-7619-3927-X (cloth)
ISBN 0-7619-3928-8 (paper)
  1. Children with disabilities—Education—United States. 2. Parent-teacher relationships—United States. I. Title.
LC4019.G66 2004
371.9'04—dc22

                    2003025971

This book is printed on acid-free paper.

04 05 06 07 10 9 8 7 6 5 4 3 2 1

Acquisitions Editor:	Robert D. Clouse
Editorial Assistant:	Jingle Vea
Production Editor:	Denise Santoyo
Copy Editor:	Toni Williams
Typesetter:	C&M Digitals (P) Ltd.
Indexer:	Kathy Paparchontis
Cover Illustrator:	Arielle E. Dubowe
Cover Designer:	Michael Dubowe

CONTENTS

Preface	ix
Acknowledgments	xi
About the Author	xiii
1. Generating Alliances, Not Lawsuits	1
Gaining Cooperation	2
Developing Alliances	3
Being Empathic	5
Communicating Well	6
Communicating Poorly	7
Staying Out of Court	9
Keeping Your Focus	12
Reflecting on Your Teaching	12
Summary	13
2. Dealing With Anger	15
Entering the Conflict Stage	16
Understanding Anger	17
Being Aware of Cultural Differences in Anger	19
Dealing With the Openly Angry Parent	20
Dealing With the Parent Who Is Always Angry	21
Dealing With the Narcissistic Parent	21
Ensuring Your Safety	22
Main Principles for Dealing With Anger	24
Principle 1: Remain Calm	24
Principle 2: Be Specific	24
Principle 3: Agree	25
Principle 4: Be Kind	25
Other Strategies for Dealing With Anger	26
What to Avoid	28

Dealing With Anger . . . Yours	28
Going Beyond Anger	30
Reflecting on Your Teaching	31
Summary	31

3. Dealing With Denial **33**

Understanding Denial	34
Discriminating Between Denial and Defensiveness	36
Dealing With Differences of Opinion	38
Knowing When Denial Is Harmful (and When It Is Not)	39
Main Principles for Dealing With Denial	40
Principle 1: Wait	40
Principle 2: Ask Why	41
Principle 3: Encourage and Exhort	42
Other Strategies for Dealing With Denial	43
What to Avoid	44
Going Beyond Denial	45
Reflecting on Your Teaching	45
Summary	46

4. Dealing With Dissatisfaction **47**

Recognizing the Context of Dissatisfaction	48
Understanding Dissatisfaction	50
Responding When Parents Reject the Individual Education Plan (IEP)	52
Coping With the Consequences of Dissatisfaction	53
Handling Mediation and Due Process Hearings	55
Main Principles for Dealing With Dissatisfaction	56
Principle 1: Focus on the Problem, Not the Person	56
Principle 2: Ask for Parents' Solutions	57
Principle 3: Stay Focused on the End Goal	58
Other Strategies for Dealing With Dissatisfaction	58
Working With Advocates	59
What to Avoid	60
Going Beyond Dissatisfaction	61
Reflecting on Your Teaching	62
Summary	62

5. Dealing With Nonparticipation and Resistance **63**

Sharing Teachers' Views	64
Discerning Noninvolvement Versus Nonparticipation	64
Understanding Nonparticipation	66
Understanding Nonparticipation of Parents of Adolescents	67
Being Sensitive to Concerns of Culturally and Linguistically Diverse Parents	69

Main Principles for Dealing With Nonparticipation
    and Resistance 69
      Principle 1: Get to Know the Parents 69
      Principle 2: Be Creative 71
      Principle 3: Confront (Listen) 72
      Principle 4: Help Parents Participate 73
Strategies for Increasing Parent Participation in Transition
    Planning 74
Other Strategies for Dealing With Nonparticipation 76
Other Strategies for Dealing With Resistance 77
What to Avoid 79
Going Beyond Nonparticipation and Resistance 80
Reflecting on Your Teaching 80
Summary 81

6. **Dealing With Mistrust** **83**
Recognizing the Value of Trust 84
Understanding Mistrust 85
Acknowledging Other Reasons for Parental Mistrust 87
Agreeing on an Individual Transition Plan 89
Preventing Mistrust 91
Main Principles for Dealing With Mistrust 93
      Principle 1: Acknowledge Mistrust Openly 93
      Principle 2: Make Amends 94
      Principle 3: Find Common Ground 94
Other Strategies for Dealing With Mistrust 95
What to Avoid 96
Going Beyond Mistrust 97
Reflecting on Your Teaching 97
Summary 97

7. **Working With Nontraditional Families** **99**
Working With Grandparents 100
    Custodial Grandparents 100
    Secondary Caregivers 102
    Not-So-Secondary Caregivers 103
Working With Noncustodial Parents 104
Working With Foster Parents 105
Working With Homeless Families 107
Working With Families Where You Suspect
    Child Abuse or Neglect 110
Reflecting on Your Teaching 113
Summary 114

8. Cultivating Collaborative Relationships	115
Resolving Your Reservations	116
Applying Cultural Considerations	118
Starting at the Beginning	120
Building Credibility	120
Using Helpful Interpersonal Skills	121
Motivating Parents	122
Defining Roles	123
Maintaining the Relationship	124
Holding Parent–Teacher Conferences	124
Conducting IEP, ITP, and Other Large Group Meetings	128
Handling Conflicts	130
Dealing With Homework	130
Establishing Boundaries and Other Support Systems	132
Passing the Torch	134
Getting and Giving Feedback	134
Recruiting Parent Mentors	134
Promoting a Family-Friendly School	136
Being Realistic	137
Reflecting on Your Teaching	138
Summary	139
Resource A: Welcome Letter	**141**
Resource B: Communication Log	**142**
Resource C: Letter to Parents of Older Elementary Students	**143**
Resource D: Letter to Parents of Adolescents	**144**
Resource E: Parent Observation Sheet	**145**
Resource F: Back-to-School Letter	**146**
Resource G: Responsibilities of Team Members	**149**
Resource H: Intake Conference Letter	**152**
Resource I: Conference Summary Sheet	**153**
Resource J: Additional Resources	**154**
References	**159**
Index	**171**

PREFACE

I entered my classroom one morning to find an envelope on my desk containing a copy of a letter from a parent—to the principal—about me. The parent, a mother who volunteered in my classroom on a weekly basis, had filed a three-page complaint about me. I was shocked. And angry. And devastated. This was the first time I had ever heard about any of her concerns. I wondered why she had not talked with me about what was troubling her and worried that her accusations might have some merit. I also feared the principal's reaction and how it would affect my employment at the school.

This all occurred during my first year as an elementary school teacher, when I was consumed with ideas and responsibilities common to novice teachers. These issues ran the gamut from developing creative lesson plans, to how to effectively teach students with limited English proficiency, to trying not to lose any students on our field trip to the science museum. They did not, however, include how to work collaboratively with parents.

Other than this one instance, my interactions with parents that year were generally brief, cordial, and superficial. Over time (and with experience), I became increasingly convinced of the importance of home–school collaboration. The occasions in which I developed a solid alliance with a parent made a huge difference in my work with the child and my attitude in general. As many have noted, parents are children's first teachers and continue to teach them throughout the life span. Yet collaboration between teachers and parents is often overlooked, perhaps because it seems so challenging.

In talking with other teachers, I know that many teachers share my experiences. Many teachers stated that they generally have little *meaningful* interaction with parents. This was even true of those who teach elementary school, where parents are generally more involved in comparison to middle and secondary school. Teachers who had memorable experiences tended to recount unpleasant ones, often because they generated the deepest emotions. Most, however, wanted deeper, more productive relationships with parents, but felt that it was out of their control.

Teacher preparation programs (including my own) generally devote little attention to working with parents, so most teachers enter the profession with inadequate preparation to collaborate with parents and other caregivers. When faced with difficult situations, such as parents who complain or accuse or threaten, most teachers have no training to fall back upon. Instead, teachers find themselves coping by the seat of their pants. Even those who have taken courses about families of children with special needs may feel at a loss when confronted with parental denial and dissatisfaction. Indeed, dealing with parents of students with special needs presents unique challenges and requires sensitivity and skill.

It is my hope that this book will fill this gap and provide a resource for educators confronted with challenging parents of students with special needs. This book is grounded in research and, just as important, grounded in real life experiences. While many of the examples are drawn from the experiences of elementary school teachers, the principles and techniques discussed are applicable across all grade levels.

This book provides tools to deal with common struggles with parents of students with special needs. Whether you encounter parents who are disengaged, parents who openly defy your teaching methods, or parents somewhere in between, this book presents information that will help you deal with parents' challenging responses. By understanding their perspectives and arming yourself with methods to address their concerns, you can move beyond conflict to true collaboration.

> By understanding their perspectives and arming yourself with methods to address their concerns, you can move beyond conflict to true collaboration.

Although this book is written from the perspective of what you as a teacher can do when faced with challenging parents, I do not mean to imply that you should bear this responsibility alone. When working with students with special needs, you are by definition part of a team of professionals and should respond as such. Communicate with your peers, enlist their support, formulate action plans together, and share responsibilities. Nevertheless, whether your particular school or team functions cohesively or does not function well at all, know that actions you take alone can produce significant results.

The first chapter, "Generating Alliances, Not Lawsuits," outlines foundational concepts, such as empathy, communication, and risk management, that underlie all parent–teacher relationships. Some of these topics will be expanded upon in greater detail in the final chapter of the book.

Chapters 2 through 6 each highlight a specific problem, such as dealing with parents who are angry or parents who are nonparticipatory. The first part of each chapter presents research and discussion to illuminate the reasons behind these problems. Several main strategies for handling parents who display these problems follow this discussion. Other approaches are also presented, and actions to avoid are clearly delineated. In keeping with the dual focus of this book—dealing with specific problems and cultivating strong relationships with parents—each of the first six chapters has a section on getting past the struggles and going beyond.

Chapter 7 focuses on working with groups that have unique concerns—grandparents, foster parents, noncustodial parents, and homeless families. In addition, child abuse reporting is discussed in the context of maintaining strong home–school relationships. Chapter 8, "Cultivating Collaborative Relationships," is devoted to an in-depth look at how to forge and maintain collaborative relationships with parents.

Throughout the book, main strategies for working with challenging parents are presented in boldface. Other approaches are highlighted by a lightbulb icon in the margin. Each chapter closes with a summary and questions for your consideration to provide an opportunity for you to examine your own professional life. Facilitators may want to use these questions and activities for group discussion. Additional resources, including sample forms and letters, can be found in the Resources section.

It is my hope that once equipped with the intervention principles and strategies presented in this book, you will find working with challenging parents of students with special needs less frustrating, less intimidating, and ultimately, more gratifying.

ACKNOWLEDGMENTS

My deepest gratitude to J. C., who has all the answers.

My heartfelt thanks

To my parents, whose sacrifice and love are unparalleled

To my husband and children, for their overwhelming support and patience

To my sisters, for always helping, no matter what the task

To the teachers and parents who shared their experiences with me

To Robb Clouse and the staff at Corwin Press who made this all possible

I also wish to acknowledge the following reviewers for their input:

Lynn Williams
Teacher
Sanchez Elementary School
Lafayette, CO

Craig Lindvahl
Teacher
Teupolis High School
Effingham, IL

Mary Ellen Somers
Teacher
Parkside Junior High School
Normal, IL

Nancy M. Moga
Principal
Callaghan Elementary School
Covington, VA

Ann Charles
Principal
Portsmouth High School
Portsmouth, OH

Jo Bellanti
Director of Special Education
Shelby County Schools
Bartlett, TN

Janine Jellander
Teacher
Mira Costa High School
Huntington Beach, CA

Robin S. Barton
Secondary Transition Specialist
Office of Special Education and
Student Services
Virginia Department of Education
Richmond, VA

Joyce Dresser
Special Needs Teacher
West Tisbury School
Tisbury, MA

Cindy L. Grainger
Special Education Coordinator
San Carlos Unified School District
Claypool, AZ

Jolanda Simes
District Mentor
for Special Education
Minneapolis Public Schools
Minneapolis, MN

ABOUT THE AUTHOR

Jean Cheng Gorman, Psy.D., is a licensed psychologist and the author of *Emotional Disorders and Learning Disabilities in the Elementary Classroom: Interactions and Interventions* (2001). After teaching in urban and suburban elementary schools, she obtained her doctorate in child and school psychology at New York University. Her interests in collaborating with parents have included research on Chinese methods of parenting as well as culturally sensitive parenting programs. Other professional interests include working with children who are medically fragile and enhancing parent–child relationships in infancy and early childhood. She currently lives with her husband and two children in Northern California.

**CORWIN
PRESS**

The Corwin Press logo—a raven striding across an open book—represents the union of courage and learning. Corwin Press is committed to improving education for all learners by publishing books and other professional development resources for those serving the field of K–12 education. By providing practical, hands-on materials, Corwin Press continues to carry out the promise of its motto: **"Helping Educators Do Their Work Better."**

GENERATING ALLIANCES, NOT LAWSUITS

"*I had parents understand that if we both were to help their children that they, the parents, needed to be on the same side as the teacher—to work together in educating and disciplining.*"

Judith Mitrani
Retired
30 years of teaching experience
New York, NY

The great majority of educators choose teaching because they enjoy working with children and may even feel more at ease with children and adolescents than with their parents (Hancock, 1998). Trained in ideology, pedagogy, methodology, and the most innovative approaches to teaching youth, educators may be surprised at their comparative lack of skills in dealing with parents. Though accustomed to students' problems and teaching dilemmas, teachers may be baffled by obstacles presented by their students' parents. Despite their good intentions, teachers may find their actions questioned, challenged, or even sabotaged by difficult parents.

At the same time, home–school collaboration is increasingly emphasized. For example, the 1997 amendments to the Individuals With Disabilities Education Act (IDEA, 1997) include specific mandates related to increased parent and family involvement. In addition, the school-to-adult life transition initiative stresses collaboration between secondary schools, the family, and the community (Wehman, 1990). Despite already demanding work responsibilities, teachers are being challenged to find ways to boost parent involvement. Having parents in the classroom may seem like more work than it is worth, particularly when teachers feel their attention must be given to the parents rather than the students. Indeed, "it needs to be recognized that parental involvement is actually a very demanding form of curriculum development for a class teacher" (Hancock, 1998, p. 410). Other means of collaborating with parents may be unfamiliar or unclear.

GAINING COOPERATION

Life (and teaching) would be much easier if you taught in a vacuum. But the fact is parents, particularly parents of students with special needs, significantly impact the outcomes of your teaching. You may instruct your students using a certain approach to learning. A parent may disagree and negate your efforts. For example, toward the end of the school year, one mother of a sixth grader with attention deficit hyperactivity disorder (ADHD) felt her son's teacher had been unfair toward her child. As a result, she told her son that he did not need to do any more homework for the remainder of the year, since he had done enough to get a good grade, and he happily complied. Conversely, joint efforts with a parent may lead to a child persevering rather than giving up. The bottom line is we could all use a little help. Wouldn't it be reassuring to know that you have more than 30 teaching partners for your students instead of feeling solely responsible for educating 30 children? Gaining cooperation, particularly from parents who are the most difficult, has direct benefits for your students—and for you.

Obstacles to cooperation can be found on both sides of home–school relationships. Parents may display hostility and mistrust, which immediately impede collaboration. Defensiveness and denial can also make cooperation difficult. Furthermore, dissatisfaction with the teacher, with services for their child, or with the school overall can taint interactions with educators. Noninvolvement, whether actual or perceived, is also a barrier. At the same time, teachers may be resistant to working with parents due to time pressures, may be insensitive to parents' concerns, and may unwittingly alienate parents.

DEVELOPING ALLIANCES

Merriam-Webster's Collegiate Dictionary (2003) defines *alliance* as "an association to further the common interests of the members." A parent–teacher alliance can be considered as a productive working relationship, deliberately formed to achieve shared goals. The type of alliance you develop with your students' parents depends upon your teaching style and personality. Some educators welcome volunteers in the classroom on a daily basis. For others this might feel disruptive or stressful. Some may prefer to use parents more as consultants for their individual children, seeking guidance for best approaches to their children's struggles. Still others would like parents to be primarily *swing-shifters,* reinforcing concepts learned in school when the children are home through the use of supplemental materials and by using similar teaching approaches.

Whether you have a strong preference for one of the above approaches or would like to engage in a balance of all three, you will need to develop good relations with your parents. This means treating them as equal partners in educating your students. Many parents take offense at being treated like aides who exist to photocopy and collate. Clearly, the classroom is your domain, and you do not need to pretend that it is not. Be up front and honest with parents early in the school year. You might explain your teaching style and then state, "I've found what works best for my students is to have parents be actively involved in the classroom on a daily basis (or reinforce concepts at home or whatever your preference is)." Being forthright in this manner enables parents to know what you expect of them. Their response also provides you with crucial information on whether they will easily follow your lead or have other plans.

Regardless of the type of partnership you form, the most effective parent–teacher alliances are characterized by the following:

♦ Mutual respect
♦ A clear understanding of one's own role
♦ A clear understanding of the other's role
♦ Opportunity for feedback
♦ Openness to change or adjustment as needed
♦ Similar expectations
♦ Defined common goals

Giving attention to each of these areas early in your relationship sets the stage for productivity throughout the school year. By the same token, ignoring or overlooking any of these areas will likely cause problems and hinder your effectiveness.

Consider the following scenario. In the hectic rush of the beginning of school, Abigail, a fourth-grade teacher, forgets to send out a welcome letter to parents (a sample letter can be found in Resource A). She meets a few parents at Back-to-School Night and sees a couple more as they drop off their children, but has little contact with the majority of her students' parents. Three months into the year, an incident occurs in which one child hurts a peer. Rumors quickly spread, and soon she is barraged with calls from worried parents seeking reassurance and from others condemning her for failing to properly supervise her students. Because this is the first contact Abigail has had with many parents, there is little history to contradict the rumors. Had she proactively contacted parents in the beginning of the school year and made periodic contact with them, at least some of the parents would have known that Abigail is an experienced teacher, very conscientious and skilled in classroom management. In all likelihood, this information and respect would have quickly squelched the damaging rumors.

A less drastic situation also illustrates the need to define the relationship early on. Mark, a seventh-grade math teacher, is accustomed to having parents volunteer in the classroom but lets them determine what they would like to do. Some immediately inform him of their preferences, while others are less assertive and wait in the wings. Seeking to put one hesitant parent at ease, he suggests that she help collate some worksheets. The parent never returns, offended that "all I did was staple." Had Mark explained his approach to parent volunteering to the parent, this unfortunate interaction would likely not have occurred.

Perhaps you enjoy mutual respect with your students' parents and your relationship has been defined and agreed upon at the outset, yet there is no established method for communicating feedback. Should a conflict arise (more likely than not), this oversight could endanger what you have worked hard to establish. Many people, whether teachers or parents, are uncomfortable with conflict and confrontation. Failing to address underlying conflict, or addressing it in such a way as to escalate it, may cause irreparable damage to the relationship. For example, Catherine, a special educator, enjoyed the respect and classroom involvement of many of her students' parents. One parent, who volunteered on a weekly basis, became bored of her role as a one-on-one reader but was not sure how to approach Catherine, since they had agreed to her job description months ago. As a result, she was increasingly dissatisfied with volunteering, which Catherine noticed as well. Neither was comfortable with openly discussing her concerns. Although nothing disastrous occurred, both teacher and parent missed out on a potentially more rewarding experience.

Ideally, both teacher and parent should feel comfortable talking directly to each other on an informal basis. Some other avenues for giving and receiving feedback can include a volunteer communication notebook, where parents can leave you comments on their experiences during the day (noting whether they would like to talk with you further), and scheduled feedback times. This does not have to be overly demanding of your time, but can be as simple as making sure to ask parents how they are feeling after a specific number of volunteering days or a certain amount of time has elapsed.

Similar expectations of what can be accomplished and a well-defined common goal are equally important. Consider selecting targets from the student's Individualized Educational Program (IEP) and using the mastery criteria defined on the plan. Having quantifiable ways to monitor progress helps both you and the parent to see the results of your efforts. More in-depth discussion of effective partnerships with parents will be covered in greater depth in Chapter 8, "Cultivating Collaborative Relationships."

BEING EMPATHIC

It is relatively easy to be empathic when a misbehaving child looks at you with puppy dog eyes, regardless of the infraction. It is much more difficult, however, to be understanding and compassionate when an adult twice your size threatens to sue you. Yet in both situations, empathy is what leads to a restored relationship. "One might conceive, then, of empathy as a first step to providing aid—a step that turns an individual into a potential helper" (Neuwberg et al., 1997, p. 513).

Cognitively, empathy involves taking the perspective of another person, inferring his or her thoughts and feelings (Ickes, 1997). Empathy on an affective level involves experiencing emotions such as sympathy and compassion (Batson & Shaw, 1991). When working with parents, both aspects are desirable. When a parent feels understood, he or she becomes more open to working with you. It is possible to understand another's motives and rationale, but feel absolutely no warmth toward them. Yet it is often the emotional component that reigns (Kerem, Fishman, & Josselson, 2001). Parents may conclude that you do not fully comprehend their view, but desire to help. As a result, they are willing to give you the benefit of the doubt and to work together. In this sense, empathy underlies cooperation.

How can you empathize with parents who complain, badger, make excuses, and generally make your life difficult? The vast majority of parents

> When a parent feels understood, he or she becomes more open to working with you.

love their children and are doing the best they can to raise them well. "It's not as if they purposely raised a child who can't or won't learn or tried to bring up a child to break all the rules in the book" (McEwan, 1998, p. 43). Certainly teaching students with special needs is challenging. Imagine parenting a child with special needs, trying your best to do what is right for your child. Yet whenever something goes wrong with your child (even when the child becomes an adult), someone will blame you—"What's his home life like," "It's because they never discipline him at home," and so forth. Now picture all of the difficult student behaviors you encounter as a teacher—disorganization, aggressive behavior, forgetfulness, and the like—and imagine dealing with them in the context of a family. Instead of a disorganized desk, there is a disastrous bedroom. Instead of aggression toward a peer, there is aggression toward an infant sibling. While some families report that their child's disability minimally affects their family life, many feel the need for parent counseling and training as well as for practical support (Leyser & Dekel, 1991). Parents of children with learning disabilities and children with behavior problems have also reported greater stress and emotional strain (Lardieri, Blacher, & Swanson, 2000). Being a parent is probably the most difficult but important job there is, but most parents do not have a support staff to help them.

COMMUNICATING WELL

The importance of communication in developing and maintaining good relationships with parents cannot be underestimated. For example, one study found that 40 *seconds* of speaking could distinguish between professionals with and without prior malpractice claims (Ambady et al., 2002). The rudiments of good communication will serve you well. "Communication in this sense means the capacity to listen, pay attention, perceive, and respond verbally and nonverbally . . . in such a way as to demonstrate to [the parent] that one has attended, listened and accurately perceived" (Okun, 1992, p. 23). Helpful verbal behaviors include

- ◆ Asking open questions
- ◆ Being an active listener
- ◆ Clarifying thoughts
- ◆ Responding to the primary message
- ◆ Summarizing important points

Nonverbal behaviors, such as maintaining good eye contact, occasional head nodding and smiling, and an open posture, are also important.

Communicating well also requires that you accurately receive the parents' communication. Nonverbal clues tend to be more reliable than verbal ones. A parent may greet you saying, "It's good to see you," but a tense stance, rigid posture, and fidgeting hands indicate otherwise. You would be wise to note that the parent is stressed and to try to discover why to put him or her at ease. Hearing verbal messages involves attending to the cognitive content (what is said) as well as the affective content (feelings and attitudes) that may be less apparent (Okun, 1992).

Focusing on one major theme at a time is an effective way to address the cognitive content. For example, a parent may approach you saying, "I'm worried about Jessica's reading. She's falling behind; it's making her frustrated and her friends are teasing her." Choose one area— Jessica's specific reading skills, lack of progress, emotional well-being, or her peer relation-

Hearing verbal messages involves attending to the cognitive content (what is said) as well as the affective content (feelings and attitudes) that may be less apparent.

ships—and discuss it in depth. However, responding only to the words expressed may result in missing an equally important hidden message. This does not mean that you should play the role of a therapist, attempting to get the parent to explore his or her feelings, but that you should be aware of the emotions behind the thoughts and respond accordingly.

Consider the following parent statement: "I don't know why it is so hard to get someone to do something around here. All I'm asking is that someone tell me what's going on with getting accommodations for my child's testing." You could respond in several ways. Focusing only on the verbal message, you could reply, "Ask the special education director, she's in charge." Although the statement is accurate and points the parent in the right direction, it is likely to increase the parent's anger because it ignores the affective element. Responding only to the parent's emotions by saying, "You seem angry, do you want to talk?" is also not appropriate, because it overlooks the parent's legitimate request. Giving weight to both aspects produces a response that will make the parent feel understood and helped. You could say something like, "I know it's been frustrating to not have an answer yet. Come with me; let's see if the special education director is in her office." This response acknowledges the parent's feelings, provides support, and guides the parent to the appropriate solution. Of course, the best answer would be to acknowledge the parent's frustration and give the actual information he or she wants, if you are able to.

COMMUNICATING POORLY

Just as there are things you can do to communicate well, there are communication blunders that will hinder your alliance regardless of your good

Table 1.1 **Effective Communication Skills**	
Verbal Skills	*Nonverbal Skills*
Asking open-ended questions	Maintaining good eye contact
Being an active listener	Occasional head nodding
Clarifying thoughts	Smiling
Responding to the primary message	Keeping an open posture
Discussing one theme at a time	Observing others' nonverbal cues
Giving attention to affective and cognitive content	
Summarizing important points	

intentions. Ambady et al.'s (2002) study found that surgeons judged to be more dominant were more likely to have been sued, with dominance conveyed by "deep, loud, moderately fast, unaccented and clearly articulated speech" (p. 8). Such tones tend to convey a lack of empathy and understanding for the listener. Other verbal behaviors can also obstruct communication, such as

♦ Using jargon
♦ Blaming
♦ Interrupting
♦ Displaying a patronizing attitude

Nonverbal behaviors such as sitting far away, checking the time, or looking away communicate disinterest and a lack of concern for the parent.

> No one intends to communicate poorly, but realistically fatigue, stress, frustration, and anger sometimes get the best of us.

No one intends to communicate poorly, but realistically fatigue, stress, frustration, and anger sometimes get the best of us. In response to the parent's request above, it is conceivable that one might say out of frustration, "Look, I'm doing the best I can. Your child isn't the only student I have, you know!" These types of statements should be avoided at all costs. They cannot be retracted and may do irreparable damage to the relationship with the parent. If you think the only response you can produce is one of exasperation, use this response instead: "Thanks for your input." Collect yourself and try talking with the parent at a later date.

Table 1.2 Poor Communication Skills	
Verbal Skills	*Nonverbal Behaviors*
Speaking loudly and rapidly	Sitting far away
Using jargon	Checking the time
Blaming	Looking away
Interrupting	Displaying a closed posture (e.g., crossed arms)
Being patronizing	Working on an unrelated task (e.g., grading papers)
Talking instead of listening	Avoiding others

One of the worst communication offenses is not communicating at all. While you may not actively try to avoid interacting with parents, it is easy to limit your encounters to required parent–teacher conferences. Because your contacts occur only during these formal conferences, your working relationship is restricted. Opening the lines of communication through brief frequent contacts helps build your relationships with parents. A time-effective way to do this would be to ask each student to provide a few self-addressed envelopes at the beginning of the school year. During the year, you can mail a quick note to the parents, informing them of some accomplishment the student made that day or other positive occurrences. Parents will know that you are thinking of them and taking note of the good (not just the bad) for their child.

STAYING OUT OF COURT

What statement raises more dread than "Indoor recess today"? When an angry parent sputters, "You'll be hearing from my lawyer!" In today's litigious society, it is quite possible that you could be involved in a lawsuit. Teachers have been successfully sued for a host of seemingly innocuous things. "The bad news is that the number of lawsuits are growing, the amount of compensation asked for by plaintiffs is rising, and even the most conscientious of teachers can make a single, momentary mistake which could result in a successful lawsuit against them" (Greene, 1998, p. 3).

Faced with such ominous news, you may feel like the resource room teacher who felt her "hands were tied" and that she needed to protect herself. Her policy with difficult parents was to never meet with them alone, so as not to "open myself up to lawsuits." Thankfully, there are many actions you can take to limit your liability, all of which will strengthen your relationships with parents rather than constrain them.

> There are many actions you can take to limit your liability, all of which will strengthen your relationships with parents rather than constrain them.

Lessons can be gleaned from the medical profession, notorious for its malpractice liability. Overall patient dissatisfaction, not just with the outcome of their treatment, has been found to lead to lawsuits. Specifically, physicians who received more complaints from patients were also more likely to be sued for malpractice (Hickson et al., 2002a). Shorter office visits and patients' feelings of being rushed or ignored are also associated with malpractice risk (Levinson, Roter, Mullooly, Dull, & Frankel, 1997; Hickson et al., 1994). The common factor in these studies is the patients' discontent, a concept that transfers easily to parents' satisfaction with their children's education. Dissatisfaction with relationships with school professionals, not just with the child's poor academic achievement, can contribute to the likelihood of litigation or similar legal proceedings (e.g., impartial hearings). Leading medical researchers assert that "Good doctoring requires time to involve patients, ask open-ended questions, identify needs, and respond appropriately" (Hickson et al., 2002b, p. 1586). The same can be applied to teachers and parents.

Beyond those basics, being savvy about risk management also lessens your vulnerability to being sued. These general principles should be evident in your classroom and dealings with parents:

1. *Document everything.* Every conversation you have with a parent, whether it is a formal meeting, a phone call, or a chance encounter, should be documented. Consider making a communication log for your class, such as a three-ring binder with a page for each student. Have columns for the date, time, and format (e.g., phone call) of your conversation as well as for the content. (A sample is provided in Resource B.) Be careful to record the facts of the encounter only. Do not put in writing any of your feelings, hypotheses, or otherwise subjective information. Keep in mind that the Family Educational Rights and Privacy Act (FERPA) of 1974 (also known as the Buckley Amendment) gives parents and students the right to inspect and review any official educational records, files, and data directly related to their children (LaMorte, 1996). FERPA excludes "private notes" from the definition of educational records (Jacob & Hartshorne, 1991), so a communication log is not likely to be inspected by parents. However, it may be called upon in event of a dispute. It is useful for reminding both the parent and the school what has been discussed and decided.

2. *Focus on the truth.* Educators can be accused of slander and libel, or oral and written communications that wrongfully defame the character of another person. "The burden of proof is on the person who made the libelous or slanderous statements" (Greene, 1998, p. 8). It is important to focus on specific verifiable facts. For example, rather than state that the child is unmotivated, it is better to state that a student failed to complete 80% of homework assignments. By the same token, do not repeat questionable information or otherwise engage in gossip. In all likelihood, such rumors will escalate and find their way to their subject.

3. *Go to the source.* Along the same lines as focusing on the truth, it is important to speak directly to important parties whenever possible. Do not rely on another teacher or administrator to carry your message for you, and do not accept crucial information from a third party. For example, assuming that a parent is in agreement with the team's recommendations because a colleague told you so may lead to trouble. If it directly impacts you, confirm it with the parent.

4. *Get help.* Do not attempt to address any conflicts with parents by yourself. Ideally, you would already be comfortable interacting as part of a team based on your experiences with student study teams or IEP/ITP (individual transition plan) teams. As early as possible, involve another professional who can help, such as the special education director. Ask your colleagues for corroborating information (being careful not to engage in slanderous discussions, of course). Inform your principal or administrator of conflicts that you believe may escalate. In addition, "speak to those individuals who can help your case or who have a clear understanding of the situation and how it occurred" (Greene, 1998, p. 15).

5. *Be professional at all times.* Resist the temptation to let down your guard and to speak off the record with parents. This includes complaining about other staff members or work conditions. Things said in these types of situations have the potential to be used against you. For example, the comment, "The new principal is a little disorganized," may be true and may account for some of the problems you are experiencing, but it does not build the parent's confidence in the school or, for that matter, in you. Seemingly innocuous but unprofessional comments only raise the possibility in parents' minds that you are unprofessional in other ways and at other times. It is also very difficult to regain your professional demeanor if the parent has already interacted with you in more informal ways.

6. *Build relationships conscientiously.* Ultimately, people who like you do not sue you. Build relationships with as many parents (and staff) as possible. Do not discount some relationships as unimportant. You never know whose support you will need or who will provide opposition in the future.

These general principles of risk management can be applied to all areas of teaching. Books such as Dunklee and Shoop's *The Principal's Quick-Reference Guide to School Law* can provide teachers with more detailed information on specific legal matters.

KEEPING YOUR FOCUS

With all of this discussion on litigation and conflicts with parents, it is easy to forget why home–school collaboration is important. Although there are benefits for both parents and teachers, ultimately, it is for the kids.

> When parents and teachers form home-school partnerships, children are more likely to see a unified front. . . . Children are free to ask their parents for guidance or help without worrying whether Mom or Dad agrees or disagrees with how the teacher teaches. . . . When school and family unite in a partnership for children, their overlapping spheres of influence (Epstein, 1995) foster a positive attitude . . . that helps children learn . . . at school. (Ford, Follmer, & Litz, 1998, p. 312)

In addition to improved attitudes, research has found that parent involvement is associated with students' greater academic achievement, such as in reading (Hewison, 1988), as well as better homework habits (Epstein, 1985, 2000). Furthermore, parent involvement may mitigate the effects of poverty and prevent dropping out of school (Epstein, 1991; Henderson & Berla, 1996).

Chances are you do not teach for money, fame, prestige, or power. You spend your time and energy preparing, talking, explaining, creating, and instructing, all in the hopes of helping children grow and flourish. Parents do too. Educators and parents hope for and are working toward the same goal.

REFLECTING ON YOUR TEACHING

For many teachers, actively building alliances with parents is new territory. Use the following questions and activities to reflect on your own teaching and guide you in working collaboratively with challenging parents of students with special needs.

1. What role do you expect parents to play in their children's education? Does this differ for parents of students with special needs?

2. How do you feel about having parents observe or volunteer in your classroom?

3. How do you normally treat parents? As consultants? As helpers? As swing-shifters?

4. What are your preferred ways of communicating with parents? Do parents know how to use these ways to reach you?

5. When was the last time a parent gave you feedback about your teaching?

6. Identify one tangible step to improve your communication with or relationships with parents of students with special needs.

SUMMARY

Working with parents is not only prudent, it is part and parcel of working with students with special needs. The type of alliance, or productive working relationship, you form with parents depends largely on your teaching style and preferences. All successful relationships, however, are characterized by mutual respect, a clear understanding of roles, an opportunity for feedback, openness to change or adjustment, similar expectations, and a defined common goal. Being empathic and communicating well are also important. Among the obstacles to strong alliances put forth by parents are hostility, mistrust, denial, and a lack of involvement. Teachers may also alienate parents due to time pressures and insensitivity. Adherence to risk management principles reduces the likelihood that litigation will result from strained relationships with parents. These include maintaining documentation, focusing on the truth and the source of information, seeking help, being professional, and actively building relationships.

DEALING WITH ANGER

"I broke up the fight and called Linda's mom to tell her what had happened. Mom started cursing and said I had always disliked her kids, and she was going to come to the school and shoot me."

Donna-Jean F. Wosencroft
K–5 Literacy Coach
30 years of teaching experience
Providence, RI

While you may not have been threatened with physical violence, undoubtedly you have encountered parents who are angry. Sometimes parents are justified for being upset; other times they are not. Although it can be, a parent's anger or hostility is not necessarily an indication of an unsuccessful parent–school relationship. Actually, conflict in relationships is to be expected as a normally occurring stage in any relationship.

ENTERING THE CONFLICT STAGE

Though not immediately evident, a teacher–parent relationship constitutes a group. Groups naturally progress through stages as they develop. Bruce W. Tuckman identified five stages that groups pass through, which he labeled forming, storming, norming, performing, and adjourning (Tuckman, 1965; Tuckman & Jenson, 1977). Although the duration of each stage varies with each group, the progression of stages does not.

During the first stage, forming, groups go through an orientation process in which there is mild tension and guarded polite interactions. In this stage, you and the parent are unfamiliar with one another and unsure of your roles. Over time, these initial inhibitions subside and the individuals begin to function together as a group. At this point, some conflict occurs, propelling the group into the next stage, storming. Changing some minor factor, such as how to communicate or when to meet, easily solves some conflicts. Minor disagreements that have not been resolved can escalate, resulting in conflict that seriously disrupts the group.

Unfortunately, many groups get mired in the storming stage, due to reluctance to openly deal with conflict or an inability to resolve conflict. For example, it may seem easier to ignore and endure the conflict you have with a parent. After all, you will only have to deal with the student and parent for the remainder of the school year. However, failing to address a parent's anger not only shuts down your relationship with that parent, it may also jeopardize your ability to work with other parents, since others are likely to find out about such a significant discord. Groups that fail to address conflict never become productive and may even dissolve. In contrast, conflict can promote group unity by allowing participants to openly discuss issues and resolve disagreements.

If conflict can be resolved, the group is able to progress to the norming stage, in which groups begin to bond tightly. There is a feeling of group unity and camaraderie. This cohesiveness allows the group to enter its productive phase, performing. At this stage, the group is mature; members are comfortable with one another and are able to engage in the group's goals. This is the enjoyable stage at which teachers and parents find they are able to make significant progress, rather than having to deal with relationship issues. The last stage, adjourning, can occur when the group accomplishes its goals or when time and resources are exhausted.

Many parent–teacher relationships stay at the forming stage—polite interactions with little work actually accomplished. "Low levels of conflict in a group could be an indication of remarkably positive interpersonal relations, but it is more likely that the group members are simply uninvolved, unmotivated, and bored" (Forsyth, 1990, p. 80). Limited time and multiple work responsibilities may hinder your efforts to deepen relationships with parents. Conflicts, however, should not be a deterrent.

When you experience conflict with a parent, keep in mind that neither of you is to blame. Rather, as a natural occurrence in all groups, you and the parent were bound to disagree over something. Treat conflict as a sign that you and the parent are on the brink of a more meaningful and productive relationship. Use the conflict to move your relationship forward, rather than allowing it to derail you from your joint goals.

> Use the conflict to move your relationship forward, rather than allowing it to derail you from your joint goals.

UNDERSTANDING ANGER

While conflicts with parents are many and varied, often the most difficult ones to resolve are those in which the parent is angry, hostile, or aggressive. The term *anger* is typically used to describe an individual's internal emotional experience, which can range in intensity from mild annoyance to fury. In contrast, hostility is "distinctly 'other-directed,' and centers on the relational implications of . . . anger" (Martin, Watson, & Wan, 2000, p. 871). A parent who is angry may grimace. One who is hostile may accuse or threaten you. The term *aggression* is reserved for behavior such as striking someone. This distinction is important insofar as it helps you distinguish between the parent who is upset versus the parent who poses actual danger to you. Most parents are angry, some are verbally hostile, and a very few are actually aggressive.

One of the most common sources of anger is being attacked by another person (Taylor, Peplau, & Sears, 1997). Blaming, insulting, and teasing are all causes of anger that can be viewed as personal attacks (Törestad, 1990). Parents may experience being attacked if they feel school professionals are ganging up on them, such as pressuring them to accept a certain school placement for their child. Parents of students with special needs may be particularly angered when school staff blame them for their children's problems, such as by stating that their home life is responsible for the child's acting out. Intimidating parents with educational jargon and being condescending also put parents on the defensive (McEwan, 1998). One parent felt judged by school staff for being a low-income single mother, because she did not understand all the "fancy words" they were using during an IEP meeting. She felt she could not ask questions, because that would further suggest her ignorance. Despite outwardly agreeing to all recommendations, she left the meeting furious.

Another main source of anger is frustration (Taylor et al., 1997). Frustration occurs when one is prevented from attaining a goal, such as obtaining services for one's special needs child. Parents' anger may be aroused when they feel the school does not have their children's best interests at heart. They may believe (erroneously or not) that budgetary concerns, internal politics, racism, ignorance, or indifference are to blame for their children's needs being overlooked. For example, one mother was furious that the school refused to make any accommodations for her son, who had been diagnosed with ADHD by an independent psychologist. The rationale she had been given was that the school administrator "didn't believe in ADHD." Parents may feel that the special education referral process has inordinate wait times between events (e.g., referral, testing, IEP meetings) or other roadblocks to getting help for their children. Broken promises, no matter how well intentioned, are also likely to raise frustration and anger in parents (McEwan, 1998).

Anger is most likely to result when the attack or frustration is seen as under the control of the other person, such as if it is seen as voluntary, unjustified, or avoidable. While most parents would not think that the school intentionally tried to harm them or their child, it is quite possible that they see mistakes made by the school or teacher as avoidable, thus raising their anger. For example, one mother was incensed over what she perceived to be arbitrary rules under the discretion of the school staff. Her first-grade son was being evaluated for emotional and behavior problems, and she had suggested multiple times to have him put in the same class as his twin sister, who tended to calm him down. In her eyes, the school was overlooking an obvious solution under the guise of some pie-in-the-sky ideas about twins and child development. Another mother was livid about the school's response to her 13-year-old daughter, who has diabetes. Though the girl's 504 plan specifically stated that she be allowed to consume soda, juice, or snacks to treat hypoglycemia, some teachers were preventing her from doing so because it was "disruptive" or because they felt she was being "manipulative" and "didn't really have hypoglycemia."

In addition to feeling attacked and frustrated, parents may also be angered by a failure to communicate. One example of a breakdown in communication involves the formation of a 504 plan. Section 504 of the Rehabilitation Act of 1973 is a civil rights statute that prevents, among other things, discrimination against children with "handicaps" (deBettencourt, 2002). Section 504 requires that schools provide reasonable accommodations to students who have an identified physical or medical condition that limits a major life activity (e.g., learning). Under Section 504, decisions about the student must be made by a "knowledgeable group"; written consent of the parents is *not* required, only notice (deBettencourt, 2002).

Although schools may be in compliance with the law when they create a 504 plan for a student, parents may balk at being excluded from the development process. For instance, a student with ADHD may have his or her classroom and homework assignments modified by requiring less work (and therefore less time needed to stay on task), such as by doing every second or third problem. Parents who are merely informed about this modification (perhaps by the student) might be flabbergasted at the rationale or the intervention. In some cases, students who are "no longer entitled to services under IDEA (e.g., students with learning disabilities who no longer meet IDEA eligibility criteria) may be entitled to accommodations under Section 504" (deBettencourt, 2002, p. 22). Parents of these students may be particularly confused and incensed about being excluded or having the school act without their input. Consequently, it is good professional practice to involve parents throughout the development of a 504 plan, even though the law does not specifically require it.

Furthermore, condescending school staff members and a lack of respect for parents and children can be sources of parents' anger (McEwan, 1998). For example, one mother of a third grader became furious over her daughter's poor midyear progress report, stating that it was the first time she had heard of any problems with her child's performance. Another father felt the school was patronizing, assuming he was ignorant because of his limited English ability.

BEING AWARE OF CULTURAL DIFFERENCES IN ANGER

The expression of anger appears to be dependent upon culture (Mandal, Bryden, & Bulman-Fleming, 1996). Not only do people learn to express anger differently, they also learn to interpret expressions of anger differently. For example, Indians tend to restrain negative emotions, such as fear and anger, perhaps because expression of strong negative emotions flouts social norms (Mandal et al., 1996). Asian cultures demonstrate similar inhibitions against showing the full intensity of one's anger or negative emotions in public. Matsumoto (1993, p. 120) explains, "In collective cultures, there is greater need to suppress one's emotional reactions, so as not to offend others in the group, avoiding conflict and confrontation."

This may make it difficult for others outside their culture to identify their feelings accurately. For instance, European American teachers may find it hard to identify anger or hostility in Asian immigrant parents, who may maintain a pleasant demeanor even when they are infuriated. Sensitivity to other indications of underlying anger is important. For example, a parent who abruptly changes the subject or smiles but does not respond verbally may be offended, even though he or she is not openly displaying it. Other indications may include avoidance, reducing participation, or changing to a more superficial level of interaction than previously used.

Similar cultural variation in the expression of anger is also found among ethnic groups within the United States, who may adhere to culturally accepted norms. For example, one study found that European Americans were less accurate in reading emotions in African Americans' facial expressions than African Americans were in reading emotions in European Americans (Nowicki, Glanville, & Demertzis, 1998).

There is also cultural variation in what causes an angry response. Some cultures, such as the Spanish, emphasize maintaining one's honor and reputation. In these cultures, the family's collective honor is a reflection of the reputation of each individual member (Rodriguez Mosquera, Manstead, & Fischer, 2002). Even children are expected to uphold the family honor by not drawing negative attention to themselves. Thus, a child who is disciplined for misbehavior or identified for problems at school may be seen as bringing shame upon the family. Sensitivity to this perspective is important when working with parents of honor cultures. Endeavor to frame a child's difficulties in such a way as to avoid casting a negative light on the child, which may make the parent angry with both the child and you.

DEALING WITH THE OPENLY ANGRY PARENT

At some point, you will encounter an openly angry parent, no matter how well your relationships with parents have been proceeding. Ideally, you should intervene when you first notice some frustration. It is easier to pre-vent an explosion than to contain one. Inquire about the source of the parent's frustration. Overcoming the parent's frustration at this level may be as simple as providing information, clarification, or reassurance. If you are in a group setting, such as a team meeting, and you notice the parent becoming increasingly frustrated, address the parent's frustration rather than ignore it and continue the group discussion. If you do not feel comfortable saying something directly, you can always cue a colleague to address it by asking, "Should we see if the parents have any questions?"

If you are not able to diffuse the parent's anger early on, you may find that the parent reaches a breaking point and makes an atypical display of anger. Warning signs of an imminent breaking point can include biting sarcasm, impatience, and being overly sensitive, as well as nonverbal expressions of pent-up emotion, such as agitation and clenched hands. For example, the parent may be intolerant of any signs of delay in providing information or services or may express frustration at being shuffled around from person to person. When a parent is at his or her breaking point, logical discourse may not be possible, and you may need to continue the discussion later, such as after a short break to retrieve requested materials or coffee. Preferably, this break would occur with the parent's assent, rather than imposing a time-out of sorts on the parent.

If a parent is angry and also hostile, there may have been a breach of trust and understanding. Parents may feel betrayed and lash out in response. For example, one mother burst into the main office one morning, demanding to know who was responsible for a child abuse report that had recently been filed on her and threatening to take action. When a resource teacher owned up to it and calmly explained why a report had to be filed, the parent softened. She knew this teacher had her son's best interests at heart and understood her professional responsibilities as a mandated reporter. However, she was hurt that the teacher did not tell her prior to making the report and that she had to find out when a social worker appeared at her doorstep.

Reestablishing trust can be difficult, and sometimes, it is impossible. Make amends and apologize as necessary. Take responsibility if appropriate.

DEALING WITH THE PARENT WHO IS ALWAYS ANGRY

Is it possible that some people are always angry? Yes. For many reasons, some people relate primarily to others in an angry fashion. Others experience the world through a defensive filter, seeing potential causes of anger at every turn. However, these types of parents are few.

If you should encounter a parent who seems angry or hostile all the time, and no school staff member is able to relate to the parent on a more pleasant level, there are a few approaches you can take. First, as much as possible, assume that everything you do or say will be met with anger, and do not take the parent's anger personally. Make every effort to be calm and kind, but remain businesslike in your demeanor. Keep your responses brief, to the point, and focused on action. This straightforward approach reduces the likelihood that you will say something that the parent can take offense at. It may be helpful to communicate in writing with this type of parent, such as through e-mail or letters mailed home. It is important to save copies of these communications for your own reference. Remember that it takes two people to sustain an argument. By limiting your part of the interpersonal interaction in these ways, you leave the parent no choice but to abandon his or her arguments.

DEALING WITH THE NARCISSISTIC PARENT

At some point, you may encounter a parent who behaves differently from other angry parents, one who seems to have been personally insulted by something and is unable to let it go. This parent may seem to be highly critical of everything except him (or her) self, lashing out with blame and condescension. This parent is characterized by feelings of personal superiority, an inflated sense of entitlement, low empathy toward others, and a belief that "ordinary people" cannot understand him or her. This constellation of characteristics defines narcissism (American Psychiatric Association, 1994). While this is a small group of people—less than 1% of the general population (American Psychiatric Association)—you may encounter them and be able to distinguish them by their grandiosity and extreme reactions to any perceived criticism. The intensity of their reaction may surprise you and will distinguish them from the typical parent who becomes angry. With these types of people, it is especially important to be aware of how you deliver feedback that may implicate the parents (e.g., "Your child hasn't developed any skills to control himself."). Such feedback is likely to arouse intense anger, outrage, and perhaps aggression or violence toward the source of the perceived insult (Stucke & Sporer, 2002). The potential for aggression is elevated "when people with a narcissistically inflated view of their own personal superiority encounter someone who explicitly disputes that opinion" (Baumeister, Bushman, & Campbell, 2000, p. 28).

Interacting with these types of parents requires particular finesse. How you say something is just as important as what you say. For example, telling a narcissistic parent, "I think Dylan needs more attention at home," implies that the parent is failing to provide what the child needs. This is likely to elicit anger, as well as rejection of what you have said. The parent may also turn the tables and blame you for the child's difficulties, which steers the conversation in an unproductive direction. Instead, you might ask the parent, "What do you think may be contributing to Dylan's acting-out behavior recently?" If the parent fails to identify the factor that you believe is the cause, you can also frame it as a question—"What about such-and-such?" Using questions allows the narcissistic parent to respond to the issue without feeling criticized. Remember that your goal is to elicit cooperation toward a common goal, even if it takes some fancy footwork to get there.

ENSURING YOUR SAFETY

With certain types of parents, such as some narcissistic parents, you should be aware of your own safety. Use your emotions as your guide. If you feel uneasy or wary, take steps to minimize the likelihood of harm. This also applies if you plan to meet individually with angry parents as opposed to being part of a team. Take safety precautions as needed.

Offer to meet the parent in a more public place, such as the school's main office, before going to your room. This enables you to gauge whether

Table 2.1	Safety Tips for Teachers Meeting With Parents

1. Greet the parent in a public place

2. Involve other staff

3. Position yourself to get to the door quickly

4. Keep your door open

5. Meet in a room near other staff members

6. Bring an objective party into the meeting

7. Use a cue word to alert staff if you need help immediately

8. Call security if you suspect or detect substance abuse

there may be any potential danger (e.g., if the parent is clearly hostile) and to change the venue of the meeting if necessary. Involve others, such as by politely introducing the parent to another staff member, in part so that others will know that you are meeting with an irate parent. When meeting with parents in your classroom, position yourself so you can get to the door quickly if necessary. Keep your door open. If confidentiality is needed, try to meet in a conference room (e.g., the principal's office) where others will be aware of your presence rather than in your isolated classroom.

At times, it may be wise to bring an objective party into the picture, such as another teacher or the principal. Having other people present provides a deterrent to the potentially violent parent. If you think the parent will balk at having others involved, you can explain that the person is there for you (e.g., as a note taker or as a supervisor would routinely observe employees) rather than as a participant in the meeting.

> Having other people present provides a deterrent to the potentially violent parent.

Caution should especially be exercised if you suspect that a parent is under the influence of drugs or alcohol. Both can significantly impair reasoning ability and may lower inhibitions for verbal or physical aggression in an otherwise reasonable individual. If a parent who is under the influence of drugs or alcohol becomes irate, immediately involve security personnel. It is better to err on the side of caution than to gamble with your safety. Kosmoski and Pollack (2001) suggest using a "cue word for the secretary to call authorities" as part of a schoolwide safety plan (p. 102). For example, you might use your classroom intercom to tell the school secretary, "Please tell Mr. Raven I will be late, because I am meeting with some

Table 2.2 Main Principles for Dealing With Anger
Principle 1: Remain Calm
Principle 2: Be Specific
Principle 3: Agree
Principle 4: Be Kind

parents," with *raven* being the cue word. This is unlikely to raise suspicion in the potentially dangerous parents, but clearly informs staff of your need for help. Once help arrives, terminate your meeting as graciously as possible. For example, state, "I'm sorry we need to cut this short. Let's set up another time to talk more." Reschedule your meeting, and be sure to send a written reminder in the event that the parent was too impaired to remember the interaction. Also, seek guidance about whether the parent's substance abuse is grounds for reporting suspected child neglect or endangerment.

MAIN PRINCIPLES FOR DEALING WITH ANGER

A few general principles apply to all situations where you are confronted by angry, hostile, or aggressive parents. While these principles may not be completely successful, they will help you diffuse anger in the majority of situations.

Principle 1: Remain Calm

At all times, be calm, especially if the parent is escalating. It is tempting to get into a shouting match, but it can be potentially disastrous. If the parent is shouting, speak in a normal voice, even if you have to start your sentence several times before the parent hears it. Make sure both your verbal and your nonverbal communications emanate calmness. Your posture should be nonthreatening and welcoming, your facial expression composed, and your voice controlled.

Do not feel you have to respond to every provocation or statement put forth by the parent. A parent who spews, "Just who do you think you are," is not really asking you a question, so do not give it a response. Instead, keep focused on the main issue and remain as serene as possible.

Principle 2: Be Specific

Most angry discussions are fruitless because of the use of generalities. For example, the parent charges that you ignore his or her daughter. You state that you need more cooperation. Both statements are useless and likely to raise the annoyance of the teacher and parent. Using specific statements, preferably fact-based, is much more manageable and likely to produce results. For example, rather than state you need the parent's cooperation, state that you would like the parent to initial the child's planner daily to reinforce its use in building the student's organizational skills.

Stay focused on the main concern and resist broadening the discussion to larger issues. For example, if the conference was convened to discuss a student's reinstatement after suspension, do not begin talking about the child's overall behavior problems or past infractions if the parent is already angry. Doing so is unlikely to be productive and may well take you off on tangents that will frustrate all involved. Instead, focus on the one issue you need to resolve in the most specific terms possible.

Principle 3: Agree

When dealing with angry parents, the magic words are "I agree." You can always find something to agree with, no matter what the parent is saying. Even if all you can agree with is the parent's exasperated statement, "This is ridiculous! I can't believe this is happening," you can say, "I agree." These two words are disarming and often end an angry tirade immediately. Why? Because the parent no longer has to convince you of the injustice of the situation. Saying "I agree" also reminds the parents that you are not their adversary.

> After saying "I agree," you are likely to be met with a moment of stunned silence. Seize the moment.

After saying "I agree," you are likely to be met with a moment of stunned silence. Seize the moment. Use the pause to shift the conversation to something more productive, such as a tangible step that can be taken. For example, the parent has been ranting and raving about the school's oversight, repeatedly calling for "someone to be responsible for what is happening." You interject, "I agree," and shift the discussion by saying, "We need to have a meeting with the special education supervisor. What days are good for you?"

Principle 4: Be Kind

Probably the last thing you want to do is to go out of your way to be kind to a hostile parent. Similar to using the magic words, "I agree," however, is the notion of using kindness to douse a fire. Rather than tell an angry parent, "Why don't you sit down and we'll talk about this rationally," you can kindly offer a chair and say, "Please have a seat. Can I get you some coffee?" It is hard to maintain a bad attitude and hostile feelings toward someone who is being pleasant and caring toward you.

In the immediate situation, being kind also works toward changing the angry parent's mood, which is ultimately more helpful than any other tactic. If you are attempting to elicit the parent's participation in an intervention for the student or in some other way require the parent's cooperation, focus on changing the parent's mood first rather than convincing an angry parent of your position. Research has found that people in a positive mood are more open to new ideas, are more flexible, and are better at solving problems (Bryan, Mathur, & Sullivan, 1996). An angry parent may adhere rigidly to one idea, whereas the same parent in a better mood may be open to different approaches.

In the overall scheme of your relationship, kindness in the face of parents' rudeness or anger is especially effective in reinforcing your role as a caring professional. Donna-Jean Wosencroft, a seasoned educator in Rhode Island, shares this story:

> We had one family that seemed to intimidate most people. They were pretty tough. One of the children got into a fight with a little girl. . . . Linda got jealous that a classmate of hers got a new coat, for no logical reason in her mind, and she planned on taking it. I broke up the fight and called Linda's mom to tell her what had happened. Mom started cursing and said I had always disliked her kids, and she was going to come to the school and shoot me. She even put her drunk boyfriend on and he added to the threats.

> The next day when I came to school I was very anxious all day. I didn't know if Linda's mom would come up to the school or what exactly would happen. I notified the principal and had alerted the custodians to be on the lookout for Linda's mom. It was after lunch when Linda's mom came up right behind me and scared me half to death. She said she was sorry for all the talk; she explained that she and her friend had been drinking and that she knew that I had always helped her and her daughters.

> Being kind and compassionate, especially in difficult circumstances, undoubtedly strengthens your relationships with parents.

OTHER STRATEGIES FOR DEALING WITH ANGER

Other ways to deal with antagonistic parents include reinforcing any positive parental behavior and reminding the parent that you both want what is best for the child (Boutte, Keepler, Tyler, & Terry, 1992). Saying something positive about the parent's child also helps (McEwan, 1998). Try to slow down the pace of the interaction as well, using active listening skills and deliberate pauses. It may be useful to "mentally compile a list of positive and nonthreatening responses to use during uncomfortable discussions . . . [such as] 'I can understand your concern' . . . and 'How can I help?'" (Kosmoski & Pollack, 2001, p. 101). This ensures that you are not fumbling for words when faced with an irate parent and instead helps you focus on diffusing the situation and helping the parent.

It is also helpful to "get to the point" (McEwan, 1998, p. 29). When faced with an emotionally charged parent who seems to be ranting and raving, it is particularly helpful to clarify the parent's desired outcome. McEwan suggests asking, "What do you want to see happen as a result of this conference?" You may be surprised to hear the parent say, "I just want an apology" or "I just needed someone to hear me out," rather than demand some unattainable solution. Boiling the parent's arguments down to one specific request is more manageable than trying to address every point and accusation.

> Boiling the parent's arguments down to one specific request is more manageable than trying to address every point and accusation.

This is also the case when you find yourself locked in a fruitless conversation with an angry parent. Shaun Kelly, a high school science teacher, recalls such an incident:

> Kathy missed her first quiz. This was a particularly easy quiz about the class expectations and general makeup of the room (where to locate equipment, etc.). She had received a progress report with a 0 for this quiz, and I let her know that it needed to be made up.

> [Kathy] takes the progress report home and I receive a phone call the next day. I took the call not imagining the rage I would encounter on the other end of the line. Her mother asked when I planned on arranging the makeup quiz for her daughter. Baffled by the question, I slowly explained that I'm after school everyday and that her daughter needs to decide when to come.

> This infuriated Kathy's mother. We went around in circles for many minutes about how I don't "arrange" for kids to be in my room on their own time after school and that she needs to do this on her own.

> I must have touched some raw nerves as the woman was nearly screaming at me. "You don't know how hard it is for her to see teachers after what so and so did to her in the fourth grade." I heard that type of thing for a half hour.

With parents such as this mother, it can be helpful to interrupt the circular discussion by identifying one tangible action to take. For instance, the incident above was finally resolved when "the special education teacher got the quiz from me and she did it in his room."

WHAT TO AVOID

Do not argue, no matter how tempting it may be. Arguing rarely extinguishes a parent's anger and usually only raises everyone's frustration. Do not respond to clearly inflammatory comments or other remarks intended to lure you into an argument. One teacher was infuriated when a father dismissed her carefully prepared presentation with sexist comments like, "You wouldn't understand what I'm talking about; you're a woman." However, rather than make a condescending remark in return, she retained her professional demeanor and kept the focus on the child's needs.

Try not to get defensive and to take the parent's statements personally. If the parent insists on insulting, blaming, or accusing you, do not try to refute the parent's insults point by point. If you must, you can provide specific concrete examples to counter the parent's statements, though the better approach is to ignore such negative discourse altogether and to refocus the discussion instead.

Do not try to prove that the parent is wrong and that you are right. While it may give you a small victory in the immediate sense, doing so will undoubtedly result in an adversarial relationship between you and the parent. Allow parents to "preserve their dignity" (McEwan, 1998, p. 36).

Avoid taking action when you or the parent is angry. Decisions made in the heat of the moment generally are not the best possible course of action. Defer action until you understand all of the circumstances and until all parties are calm (Kosmoski & Pollack, 2001).

DEALING WITH ANGER . . . YOURS

A red-faced parent stands before you, sputtering insults, ignoring your statements, and generally being hostile. Your first impulse is to offer some tea and cookies and to be sympathetic, right? Hardly. Facing such a parent may arouse many of the same emotions in yourself. Perhaps you want to make a sarcastic remark or otherwise display some of the anger you are feeling. Instead, take steps to reduce your anger level— count to 10, pretend the parent is wearing a chicken costume, or take deep breaths and force a smile. Nothing will be accomplished while you are angry. More likely, words will be exchanged that will later be difficult to retract.

If you find you cannot control your anger, break the exchange by excusing yourself. Ideally, you would excuse yourself in order to enlist some help—"Excuse me for a moment while I find so-and-so, who I think can help us." You can also say, "I'll be right back," and take a quick breather (or do a silent scream) to calm down. Hopefully, the parent will also calm down at the same time. Use the time to think about the one essential point that you would like the parent to take home. Return with something to offer the parent (even if it is as simple as a glass of water). Resume the discussion by acknowledging the anger and by scaling it down to the one point you have identified. Also remember to acknowledge the parent's good intentions and refocus the discussion to the child. You may say something like this:

> Thanks for waiting. Would you like some water? This situation is frustrating for everyone. Let's focus on the main issue for Tommy in class right now—he is hitting other kids. It's obvious that you love him, and we really want to help him too. Here is a list of interventions that the staff and I put together that we'd like to try. Which ones do you think would be best for him?

Dealing with your anger is also important for reestablishing your objectivity and effectiveness. Research suggests, "Those in a good mood may be better able to behave in a rational and effective way in otherwise difficult and conflict-laden situations" (Forgas, 2002, p. 20). Anger can interfere with your judgment and ability to work collaboratively both in the immediate sense and in the long term.

The two classic responses to being offended are avoidance and revenge (McCullough, 2001). Although no teachers would like to think that they actually took revenge on a parent, it may be the case that multiple negative interactions with a hostile parent lead teachers to act in ways they normally would not. For example, though Susan normally went out of her way to communicate to parents positive things her students did, with one father who repeatedly offended her, she purposely did not take the time to send a note home when his child successfully used the communication board for the first time.

More commonly, teachers may avoid parents who make them angry. While this may seem like a reasonable strategy in the short term, it will certainly harm your working relationship over time. Openly addressing your conflict with the parent may be challenging initially but is better for your overall relationship. In addition, regaining a more balanced perspective will enable you to work effectively in the long term.

One way to deal with the conflict if it cannot be resolved openly is to forgive the parent. It may seem inappropriate to mention the concept of forgiveness in a professional book for educators. However, increasing evidence shows that it is one of the best ways to deal with anger and is related to lower degrees of depression and anxiety, better self-esteem, and higher life satisfaction (see McCullough & Worthington [1999] for a review of research).

Forgiveness does not mean excusing or justifying the offender's inappropriate behavior, nor does it always include reconciliation. Instead, forgiveness is choosing to release the past and mend the present. "When people forgive, they become less motivated to harm . . . their relationship with the transgressor, and simultaneously, become more motivated to act in ways that will benefit . . . their relationship with the transgressor" (McCullough, 2001, p. 194). Frederic Luskin's (2002) *Forgive for Good: A Proven Prescription for Health and Happiness* and Robert Enright's (2001) *Forgiveness Is a Choice: A Step-by-Step Process for Resolving Anger and Restoring Hope* provide detailed information about how to forgive.

Most interactions with challenging parents do not require such a purposeful response from you. However, a few experiences, particularly those with hostile parents, may result in your being so affronted that it colors your overall relationship with the parent (and, possibly, student). Brooding about the offense tends to increase feelings of avoidance and revenge (McCullough, Bellah, Kilpatrick, & Johnson, 2001). In these situations, a specific response, such as forgiveness, may be necessary in order to free yourself from being haunted by the transgression and to move on.

GOING BEYOND ANGER

If you are able to deal openly with a parent's anger, you can harness the energy the parent has to accomplish something new. This may be the time to persuade the parent to take action, to do something productive. Anger suggests that the parent has the motivation to work toward a solution (though the parent may not be so inclined). Perhaps the parent can be the squeaky wheel at the district office that is able to obtain additional services or personnel for the school.

> If you are able to deal openly with a parent's anger, you can harness the energy the parent has to accomplish something new.

The most vociferous argumentative parent can be encouraged to be an advocate for all students with special needs. One enraged mother who felt outraged by the school's limited services for her autistic son was encouraged to do more than complain to the principal. She consequently wrote to her senator, who actually called to talk more with her. This not only reduced the mother's anger, but also changed her approach in general. She felt empowered and at the same time was more aware of the need for teamwork. Another father who felt the school did not know how to accommodate his hearing-impaired daughter embarked on a public awareness campaign, going so far as to contact the *Oprah Winfrey Show* in order to raise consciousness about the needs of young children with sensory impairment.

REFLECTING ON YOUR TEACHING

Angry parents are hard to deal with and hard to forget. Use the following questions and activities to reflect on your teaching and guide you in dealing with parents who are angry or hostile.

1. To what extent do you feel comfortable with conflict and confrontation?

2. How do you normally try to handle your anger? Someone else's anger?

3. Are you aware of and comfortable with the various ways anger can be expressed by different cultural groups?

4. Are there any parents you continue to feel anger toward although the original incident is long past? How might this impact your current relationships?

5. Do you and your school have a safety plan in place for staff members, such as a universal cue word?

6. Make a list of stock responses you can use if confronted by an angry parent.

SUMMARY

It is inevitable that you will encounter an angry parent. However, this does not necessarily mean that you (or the parent) are to blame. Rather, conflict occurs in all relationships and should be expected. General principles to remember when working with angry or hostile parents include staying calm, being specific, using kindness, and agreeing. With potentially aggressive parents, you will need to employ safety precautions, such as including others in your meetings and using cue words with school staff. It is also important to deal with your own anger, perhaps by forgiving the offending parent, in order to restore the relationship. Rather than avoid dealing with a parent's anger, you can use the conflict as an opportunity to move the relationship toward a more productive phase. Angry parents can also be encouraged to harness their energy to advocate for their children on a broader scale.

DEALING WITH DENIAL

"**W**e all (including the mother) went through [the list] and agreed that [her 7-year-old son] met all criteria. When we concluded that meeting criteria meant he had Asperger Disorder, the mother just shook her head and said no. She would not accept the diagnosis that her son met criteria for."

Laura Olson Bermudez, Psy.D.
Clinical Psychologist
San Diego, CA

"They're in denial." Chances are, either you have said this about parents of students with special needs or you have heard someone say it. Perhaps you felt the parents were in denial about their child's diagnosis or were not recognizing the severity of their children's disabilities. Quite possibly, you were right.

UNDERSTANDING DENIAL

Denial is how people cope when they have no other way to deal with an overwhelming situation. Rather than face stressful circumstances, people pretend the stressor does not exist. For example, instead of acknowledging his wife's extramarital affair, a husband may turn a blind eye to obvious signs of infidelity. A woman might avoid seeing a doctor about the lump in her breast, fearing the possibility of breast cancer. Not wanting to admit that bad things are looming over you is a natural response when you feel stressed. For many parents of students with special needs, this sense of impending doom may arise from being given negative feedback about their children, such as when their children are first diagnosed with a disability.

In some cases, parents have had suspicions about their child's "differentness" and are not tremendously surprised when initially informed of a diagnosis by professionals. This may be the case with children who have physical disabilities, such as vision or hearing loss. Other parents may have viewed their child as "normal" up until the point of diagnosis. "The process of redefining as disabled a child once defined as 'normal' appears to be a very difficult one for parents" (Seligman & Darling, 1989, p. 46).

When confronted for the first time that their child has a disability, many parents go through an emotional process similar to what happens when hearing news of serious illness or loss of a loved one. One father states, "I believe one has to come to grips with the psychological implications of dealing with an illness; dyslexia and illness produce similar stresses" (Hartwig, 1984). Many state that the stages of mourning identified by Elisabeth Kübler-Ross (1969) are similar to what they experience as parents of students with special needs. Kübler-Ross's stages begin with denial and progress though anger, bargaining, depression, acceptance, and finally hope.

Denial is characterized by feelings of confusion, numbness, disorganization, and helplessness (Seligman & Darling, 1989). When parents are faced with someone telling them that their child has a disorder, a disability, or other problems requiring formal intervention, they may understandably respond, "There must be some mistake," "Give him some time and he'll be fine," or "We'll make her work harder, and we'll help her" (Hartwig, 1984).

> During this stage, rational thought may be overwhelmed by the parents' strong emotions.

During this stage, rational thought may be overwhelmed by the parents' strong emotions. Even when confronted with a list of criteria for a diagnosis, parents may agree that the child meets the criteria, but disagree on the diagnosis. Laura Olson Bermudez, a clinical psychologist, reflects on her experience working in a public elementary school:

> I can remember sitting in an IEP [meeting] with a mother, teacher, school psychologist, and principal. It was the first time a mother would be told that her 7-year-old son met criteria for Asperger Disorder. We all (including the mother) went through and agreed that he met all criteria. When we concluded that meeting criteria meant he had Asperger Disorder, the mother just shook her head and said no. She would not accept the diagnosis that her son met criteria for.

To some parents, like this mother, the label means something more than just the criteria. Perhaps parents are unwilling to accept the ramifications of the disability. Richard Tolfo, an educator with 12 years of teaching experience, stated,

> I've heard throughout the years many stories of parents who are in denial of their children's special needs. . . . Some even refuse to allow the school to provide special ed services to their kids. It's as if by not admitting it, the problem doesn't exist. As a Filipino-American, I know firsthand the kind of expectations and pressure some parents can exert on their kids. I think it's especially hard for Asian parents to accept that their child may be special ed.

Similarly, parents may be unwilling to agree to a diagnosis because they associate a worst-case scenario with the label or have very negative views about a certain disorder. For example, one mother stated, "I didn't believe them when they said my child had mental retardation. I knew a kid who was retarded growing up—he was always shrieking and drooling—and my son isn't like that at all."

Parents who reject a diagnosis may not be rejecting the idea that their child has problems. Instead, they may be taking issue with terminology that has emotional implications for *them*. This includes parents who refuse to believe their child has a specific disability, because they also experienced similar problems as a child. For example, one very disorganized and impulsive mother resented the school's suggestion that her

> Parents who reject a diagnosis may not be rejecting the idea that their child has problems.

fifth-grade daughter be evaluated for ADHD, saying that their family was just "free-spirited."

You may also encounter parents who deny the validity of a diagnosis because they experienced similar problems as a child but were given a different explanation. For example, one father refused to believe that his third-grade son had a nonverbal learning disability, since he also had problems with handwriting and mathematics but was told that he "just needed to concentrate more." Another mother stated that she had similar behavior and learning problems as those her son was now experiencing and that her son "must be distractible like me" rather than mentally retarded. Parental guilt can also interfere with acknowledging a child's disabilities. One mother, a special education teacher, could not believe when her son was diagnosed with a reading disability. In disbelief, she wondered, "How could I have overlooked that?"

DISCRIMINATING BETWEEN DENIAL AND DEFENSIVENESS

Sometimes denial is actually defensiveness. For example, when a mother refuses to hear negative information and repeatedly stresses what her child *can* do, she may not be denying the existence of problems, but reacting to what she perceives as devaluation of her child. In Lake and Billingsley's (2000) study of the factors that contribute to parent–school conflict in special education, discrepant views of a child or a child's needs were identified in 90% of situations of escalating conflict. Most often, parents complained that the school focused on the child's weaknesses or did not have a picture of the whole child. One parent was quoted as saying,

> I often think if [school staff] could do one-on-one instead of [coming] with five people, telling me Susie can't do this, Susie can't do that, and Susie can't this and Susie can't that. And I am thinking, What about "Susie *can* do this and Susie can do that"? (Lake & Billingsley, 2000, p. 245)

Parents naturally become protective of their children if they think the school is being negative. You can distinguish these parents from those who truly deny their children's problems by focusing on topics the parents have raised and by saying something positive. For example, consider the following scenario.

You are meeting with a mother to discuss a student's continued difficulties in reading comprehension. After giving many examples of skills the child lacks, the mother insists that her child understands what they read together at home. Asking the mother to describe what she has seen and heard when they read together will enable you to determine if she is oblivious to the child's problems or simply feels the need to prevent her child from being viewed too harshly. Perhaps the mother will admit that the child is able to answer simple factual questions about the material but she had to help the child identify the main idea. These details would suggest the mother was merely behaving defensively rather than denying the child's continued reading problems. Also, saying something positive will often reassure the defensive parent that you see the child's strengths and weaknesses. As a result, the defensive parent is likely to feel more comfortable discussing the child's problem areas.

Parents may also behave defensively when they are presented with information that is black and white or doctrinaire. For example, one special education director was known to tell parents, "You have to accept the fact that your daughter has mental retardation and there is nothing else we can do for her." A teacher may be tempted to say, "The only way Kayla is going to improve her speech is if she gets evaluated for speech and language services." When information is presented dogmatically, parents may emotionally recoil and reject what they hear. Presenting information in such a way as to allow for consideration of others' views helps parents accept your statements. Thus, you might say, "Kayla's communication is improving with the one-on-one help the aide has been giving her, and there are a few other things—like speech and language services—you may be interested in to boost her language skills."

Similarly, rather than using statements that cast the child in a negative light, present both positive and negative facts. Instead of saying, "Casey still has trouble staying on task," state that "Casey is able to focus on instruction at the chalkboard but has difficulty during circle time." Parents would be hard-pressed to deny such specific information and are less likely to be emotionally put off by objective facts. Being sensitive in your language also helps defensive parents drop their disbelieving postures. For example, school professionals use terms such as *below average* and *learning disabled* routinely. These same terms sound dreadful to parents, especially those hearing them for the first time. Avoiding loaded terms will reduce parents' defensiveness (e.g., use "still developing his social skills" rather than "immature").

You can also distinguish between denial and defensiveness with a change in setting. Some parents feel intimidated in meetings with a large number of school professionals. Though such meetings may be necessary, they often do not allow parents to openly discuss their views and put parents on the defensive (i.e., us against them). Talking with parents one-to-one will reveal whether they truly do not agree with identified problems or were acting that way because they felt cornered in the large group setting.

Last, parents can become defensive if the problem touches on a personal issue. Isabelle, a middle school teacher, recalls an experience with the father of a 13-year-old boy, Stephen, whose sibling had been suddenly hospitalized a month prior to the incident. At the time, rumors of drug abuse in the home were rampant.

The incident occurred at a pep rally where I was chaperoning along with several other teachers. About an hour or so into the rally a student alerted me to Stephen's behavior. She indicated to me that it looked like Stephen had "had a few."

... I watched as Stephen staggered across the floor outside of the gym. . . . I approached him, and asked him to take a seat and talk to me for a while. He smelled of alcohol and had trouble focusing. Stephen got very emotional very quickly when he realized I suspected he had been drinking. . . . I asked if he might submit to a Breathalyzer, which we had on hand. I said we would do it out of the way, and if he had not been drinking that would prove it. He replied that his father advised him "never to let anyone give him a Breathalyzer!"

After an administrator and several police officers finished talking with Stephen, his father finally showed up 45 minutes or so after I initially confronted Stephen. . . . He asked Stephen to apologize to the administrator for giving her a hard time and took him home.

On Monday morning, Stephen's father agreed that Stephen probably made a poor decision on Friday night, but stopped short of admitting he thought his son was drinking.

As the week went on, repeated calls to the father to discuss Stephen's disciplinary action were unanswered. When we finally got ahold of his father, he said he wanted to fight the punishment, because we have no proof of Stephen drinking.

At the presuspension meeting, Stephen's father "cross examined" me a bit, questioning why he did not notice the same behavior when he came to pick Stephen up.

In cases such as these, parents may be responding defensively and irrationally because they cannot separate themselves from their children's issues. With these individuals, it may be wise to refrain from attempting to get them to acknowledge your perspective. Focus instead on what you need to achieve. For example, in the above situation, the school and father could agree to an internal/office suspension as well as some counseling for Stephen without necessarily sharing the same view of the incident at the rally.

DEALING WITH DIFFERENCES OF OPINION

A genuine difference of opinion may also be misinterpreted as denial. In addition to initial diagnoses, parents may refuse to acknowledge the truth of other feedback about their children. For example, many parents do not want to believe that their children are capable of egregious behavior, especially if they do not see similar behavior at home. However, the school setting differs from the home setting, and children respond differently. A child who is heavily supervised at home may not act out until he or she is in a less restrained group situation, such as in the lunchroom or on the playground, or until he or she is faced with multiple distractions and temptations (e.g., peers). Alternatively, "when the behavior in school is related to anger and rebellion against reasonable expectations, it is possible that it does not show itself at home because nothing has ever been expected of the child" (Harden, 1993, p. 41). Acknowledge the potential truth of parents' statements that "my child never does that at home." Remind parents that people behave differently in different settings and that both the parents' and your view can be accurate.

Culture also plays a role in parents' views of their children's problems. For example, one study found that many Latina mothers of children with developmental disabilities did not see their children as responsible for their behavior problems (Chavira, Lopez, Blacher, & Shapiro, 2000). Other research has shown that many traditional Hispanic families consider the label "mild learning disabilities" inappropriate if the child's social competence meets expected cultural norms (Harry, 1992b). It may be a true difference of opinion, rather than denial, that you are faced with. In these cases, you may be quite unsuccessful in changing the parents' views. Instead, consider whether you need the parent to agree with your view (e.g., the truth) in order to get what you want. For example, one woman battled breast cancer before going into remission. When told a few years later that the cancer had returned, she refused to believe it and kept trying to find a doctor who would treat her "arthritis." Finally, one creative physician agreed that she needed "treatment for her arthritis" and started her on chemotherapy immediately. The woman dutifully complied with all aspects of treatment, even though she refused to say her cancer had returned. Perhaps the parents would be willing to try your suggested intervention even if they are not willing to endorse your view of the situation.

KNOWING WHEN DENIAL IS HARMFUL (AND WHEN IT IS NOT)

In most cases, denial is short-lived and not detrimental. After parents get over their initial shock or defensiveness, they no longer deny their children's problems and are ready to address them. In other cases, denial is more protracted and can be challenging to deal with. Endeavor to identify why you (or others) are troubled by parents' denials. Perhaps a power struggle is brewing, the parents' denials are seen as further evidence of their lack of cooperation, or you believe the parent is not acting in the child's best interest. For example, parents who refuse a more restrictive special education placement for their child may cause their child to miss out on potentially helpful opportunities. These parents may be making unwise educational decisions (which may upset any conscientious educator), but they are probably not abusing or irreparably damaging their children.

However, in other cases, parents may persist in denying their children's problems to such an extent as to risk hurting their children. Some parents reject their child because of their special needs, which may result in the child's becoming emotionally insecure and unable to adjust to the disability (Lerner, 1993). For example, the parents of one girl who had serious learning disabilities and emotional problems repeatedly refused to acknowledge their daughter's disorders and instead pushed for her to attend the most academically advanced program in the district. Not only was the program beyond the child's intellectual ability, the parents' unrealistic expectations only served to reinforce her negative self-image and depression. Another father would not believe that his son had dyslexia and insisted that he participate in a myriad of activities that his three older siblings had engaged in when they were his age. In this family of overachievers, the child with special needs was the one black sheep, which was eventually manifested in his behavior problems (e.g., truancy and substance abuse). Though it may be challenging to be empathic with these parents, recognize that parents who are hurting their children with their denial have no better means to handle their life circumstances. Maintaining a nonjudgmental attitude will help you gradually sway parents toward recognizing the truth.

MAIN PRINCIPLES FOR DEALING WITH DENIAL

 As educators, it may be frustrating to deal with parents' denial, since the truth may seem obvious and indisputable. It is important to expect denial, particularly when presenting any significant information to parents. Keeping the three following principles in mind will enable you to effectively deal with this type of resistance from the outset.

Principle 1: Wait

When parents are presented for the first time with information about their child that is significant or negative, they often need time to absorb the news and its implications. Give them some time to process what you are saying, both emotionally and cognitively. For example, one couple thought that their 4-year-old son had some developmental delays and respected their pediatrician's advice to have him evaluated. During the feedback session, the parents were presented with a detailed report on their son's

Table 3.1	Main Principles for Dealing With Denial
Principle 1: Wait	
Principle 2: Ask Why	
Principle 3: Encourage and Exhort	

abilities, including the diagnosis that their son had autism. Recalling that meeting, the mother stated, "After I heard the word, autism, I just stopped hearing. I don't remember anything else they said. It was all I could do to keep from crying in front of everyone."

Give information in small doses to allow parents the opportunity to ask questions. Psychologist Olson Bermudez states that denial may serve a "functional purpose for a parent in allowing them to process and accept information at their own pace. . . . Sometimes many 'seeds' need to be planted before they can accept reality" (L. Olson Bermudez, personal communication, October 15, 2002). Wait until they are more psychologically able to absorb what you are presenting to discuss issues that require making decisions.

Principle 2: Ask Why

It is important to understand why a parent refuses a diagnosis or disagrees with your assessment of the child's problems. Genuinely inquiring about the reasons behind parents' views is essential. You may need to correct some mistaken ideas or provide information. For example, one father refused to believe that his daughter had an emotional disorder and said, "Children can't be depressed. What's there to be depressed about when you're 11 years old?" Use concrete examples whenever possible to illustrate your point and to change parents' erroneous beliefs. For instance, rather than tell parents that their son is distractible, it is helpful to use time sampling (behavior analysis) to state that the child is typically on task 23% of the time or that he engages in inappropriate behavior an average of 10 times a day.

Parents may also deny their children's problems because they feel incapable of handling the diagnosis. It is helpful to reassure parents that the impact of the child's disability may not be as devastating as they imagine. Being diagnosed with a developmental disability may sound bleak to parents who have little information or exposure to childhood disorders. Giving parents examples of other students with similar problems can make the diagnosis less threatening. For instance, you may say "One previous student of mine who also had Down's syndrome now works as a teacher's aide in a preschool classroom and loves it."

Remember that asking why means seeking to *understand* the parents' perspective, not challenging it. Asking why also ensures that your own defensiveness about the situation is not interfering with your work with the parents.

Principle 3: Encourage and Exhort

Parents who deny the severity of their children's disabilities are struggling to cope and require emotional and psychological support. "Parents reported that part of the devastation of diagnosis of disability in their children resulted from their feelings of inadequacy and inability to deal with the unique medical, educational, and daily caretaking needs of their children" (Scorgie, Wilgosh, & McDonald, 1996, p. 76). They may be overwhelmed by what it means to have a child with disabilities. "The ability of individuals to cope with any situation depends on how they define the situation. . . . Because the birth of a child with a disability is generally an unanticipated event, parents must rely on other people to establish meaning for them" (Seligman & Darling, 1989, p. 56). You can set the tone by being empathic and supportive. In Scorgie et al.'s study of parents of special needs children, parents stated that the most helpful professionals were those who were honest; gave encouragement, affirmation, and hope; allowed parents to express their emotions and to realize that these emotions were normal; helped parents discover their strengths; showed an openness to alternatives; and had knowledge of additional sources of support.

Occasional positive comments such as, "You really pour yourself into your kids" go a long way toward affirming the parent's efforts and capabilities. In addition, acknowledging the child's strengths (e.g., "I love teaching Eric. He is so funny!") is also encouraging for parents who may be inundated with negative information. Recognizing the importance of parenting and building the parents' confidence is an important part of helping parents get past denial and move toward more effective coping.

All difficult information should be given as compassionately as possible. Though honesty may be the best policy, tactfulness is vital. Rather than repeatedly press the issue, treat these parents as if you were giving bad news to a close friend or relative—very gently. Maintain an eye toward the future and any positive signs. Do not give bad news without providing possible solutions. Instead of saying, "Melanie's coordination seems to be getting worse," say "There are some new problems with Melanie's fine motor skills lately that I think we can address."

Steer parents toward support groups who can help them through this difficult time. Hearing information from other parents who have been through similar experiences is often more readily accepted than the same information provided by a school professional. Examples of support groups include Children and Adults with Attention Deficit Disorder, which holds monthly meetings nationwide, and the International Dyslexia Association, which has newsletters and fact sheets in addition to support groups. (Other resources are provided in Resource J.) Other school professionals, such as the school psychologist or counselor, may also be helpful in providing support for overwhelmed parents.

OTHER STRATEGIES FOR DEALING WITH DENIAL

By carefully planning how you will present challenging information to parents, you reduce the likelihood that they will be defensive and react with denial. Approach your *first* contact with parents with the attitude of "Please help me to better understand and help your child," rather than attempting to convince parents of your beliefs (Downing & Downing, 1991). Enlisting parents as information gatherers and observers is also more effective in swaying parents' opinions than merely telling (or showing) them a problem exists (Downing & Downing). For example, asking parents to maintain a home behavior log

> Enlisting parents as information gatherers and observers is also more effective in swaying parents' opinions than merely telling (or showing) them a problem exists.

may help open their eyes to a child's behavior problems more successfully than trying to convince them of problems you have seen at school.

Similarly, if you must assign a label (e.g., mental retardation), "invite a *process* of negotiation as . . . an opportunity for initial family adjustment" (Abrams & Goodman, 1998, p. 96, emphasis added). This allows parents to accept reality while simultaneously keeping the information tolerable.

In addition, Abbott and Gold (1991) offer the following suggestions:

1. Keep a file of samples of the child's work and behavioral observations.

2. Have dated anecdotal records to show parents.

3. Use an informal seating arrangement.

4. List the special modifications you have made in an attempt to help the child learn more effectively.

5. Ask parents to describe how the child has been doing at home.

6. Be an active listener and allow parents to express their feelings.

In two-parent families, have both parents attend the meeting to minimize confusion that may result when one parent relays information to the other (Abbott & Gold, 1991). You may notice that one parent is more receptive than the other. It can be helpful to have that parent restate the observed behaviors in his or her own words so that the other parent realizes that you are not judging them or criticizing their child (Manning & Schindler, 1997).

Always remember to use people-first language, such as by saying, "a child with special needs" rather than "special education students." This reminds you and the parent to focus on the child and not on the disability or classification.

Although it is imperative to be empathic, it is also important to maintain a firm stance about your concerns. Manning and Schindler (1997) state, "A teacher who maintains a firm, well-reasoned position can help parents overcome their own ambivalence and can be reassuring. After all, if you aren't sure, how can they be?" (p. 33).

If you vacillate about your worries, such as by downplaying the severity of the problem if parents seem upset, it makes it easier for parents to dismiss your information.

WHAT TO AVOID

When faced with parents who are in denial, it is tempting to confront them head-on. All evidence may point to a specific diagnosis or intervention, and after presenting it (for the third time), you may want to say, "You've got to face it. Eddie has a behavior problem." Resist this temptation at all costs. If a parent is truly in denial, confronting them when they are not ready may be counterproductive and detrimental. Unless you have a better coping mechanism to offer, do not shatter parents' denial. Confronting them when they are not ready

> Unless you have a better coping mechanism to offer, do not shatter parents' denial.

will only make them feel that you do not understand them or care for their child. Realize also that many parents are reluctant to accept a diagnosis presented by a teacher and that this information should come from another professional, such as a psychologist or physician (Abbott & Gold, 1991).

It can also be very frustrating to deal with parents who are in denial, especially if you believe their inability to cope with the truth is interfering with the child's progress. Keep your emotions in check and try to refrain from saying anything about the problem when you are feeling frustrated. Instead, console yourself with the fact that if the problem is substantial, it will continue to surface and there will be future opportunities to convince parents of the truth, hopefully when they are more able to accept it.

GOING BEYOND DENIAL

Kübler-Ross's (1969) stages of mourning culminate in the final stage of hope. Ideally, this is where parents of students with special needs should be. Getting parents to accept disheartening news is important, but moving beyond mere acceptance to a more positive attitude is vital. Hope is necessary not just for the parents' coping with the child's problems, but also for the child. The attitude a child adopts toward his or her difficulties is largely derived from what significant others display. If you and the parents project an optimistic view of the child's abilities and future, the child is likely to be more hopeful as well. Hope generates resilience and is part of healthy self-esteem. This will do more to help the child overcome challenges than almost anything else.

For many parents, positive reframing of the situation is critical to moving past disbelief and to a more hopeful reality (Scorgie et al., 1996). Some parents make a personal choice to be as successful as possible as the parent of a child with a disability and use information-gathering and networking to their child's advantage. Others search for purpose or meaning in their situation. As one mother commented,

> You must not forget that there is a positive side. I think having a child with special needs forces you to dig deep and learn your own resources and learn your own strengths. . . . You do give up a lot, but you also gain a lot. (Scorgie et al., 1996, p. 76)

Being the parent of a child with disabilities often requires three different roles: parent, teacher, and advocate (Scorgie et al., 1996). Helping parents become comfortable in their roles as teacher and advocate will move them past coping and toward hope.

REFLECTING ON YOUR TEACHING

As a teacher, you are accustomed to identifying problems and areas of weakness so you can instruct students accordingly. Parents, however, may not share this problem-oriented perspective and may react with denial when presented with significant or negative information about their child. Use the following questions and activities to guide you in exploring your approach to parents who may be in denial.

1. Think of a time when you were in denial about something. Why were you experiencing denial and what helped you face your problem?

2. How and when do you tend to present information to parents (e.g., in face-to-face meetings, over the phone, with sample work)?

3. How often and in what situations do you use labels when talking with parents?

4. How would you handle a parent who has a genuine difference of opinion (perhaps culturally based) about his or her child's problems?

5. Identify a student in your classroom who is experiencing difficulties. Role-play how you would discuss the issue with the student's parents.

SUMMARY

Parents who are presented with feedback about their children may be hearing significant or negative information for the first time. Their initial reaction may be denial, a natural coping strategy that helps parents process information when they are psychologically ready. Distinguishing between defensiveness, a difference of opinion, and true denial is essential for identifying whether the parent's response is actually harming the child. Avoid confronting the parent with brutal honesty and pressuring the parent to acknowledge "the truth." It is essential to be patient, present information in small doses, and wait until the parents are coping better to make important decisions. Inquire about the parents' reasons for disagreeing with your views and gently correct any mistaken ideas. Above all, provide support for parents who may be struggling emotionally and set a positive tone by modeling acceptance of the child and hopefulness regarding the future.

DEALING WITH DISSATISFACTION

"There is nothing special about special education."

Detterman & Thompson (1997, p. 1082)

Y our students complain all the time—about assignments that are too long or too hard, about not having enough free time, about not getting to sit with their friends. Students' dissatisfaction is easy to handle; you are confident about your instructional choices and know that not all wants are satisfied (e.g., not everyone can be first in line). Parents' complaints are not so easily dealt with. They may be displeased with your teaching or hold you responsible for things you have no control over. Dissatisfied parents may complain to you or may go directly to your superiors. Must all parents' wants be satisfied? After all, as one disgruntled parent put it, "My tax dollars are paying for all of this."

RECOGNIZING THE CONTEXT OF DISSATISFACTION

Multiple signs point to a growing sense of dissatisfaction with the current educational system. Most obviously, efforts to reform public education exist at the federal, state, and local levels. Some politicians have gone so far as to suggest abolishing the system as it stands (e.g., dismantling the Board of Education) or to turning over management of schools to the private sector. School choice, viewed by many parents and policymakers as the solution to current educational problems, is a clear indication that the general public expects better than they are receiving. The No Child Left Behind Act, passed in 2002, takes accountability to a higher level, requiring states to offer choices to students in schools that fail to make progress.

In addition, news stories about corruption, mismanagement, and poor decision making at the school district level are common. One example is found in the *San Francisco Chronicle's* coverage of the Oakland school district, which has the largest school district deficit in California history, estimated to be as high as $70 million (May, 2003). Columnists Matier and Ross (2003) state the following:

> After six months of fiscal finger-pointing, political infighting and personal attacks, it's pretty clear that the debate over how to solve the Oakland school system's budgetary meltdown has very little to do with money—and very much to do with power. . . . [The $17 million budget cuts] are not about helping the kids as much as they are about helping . . . [the superintendent] and the board stay in power.

Some parents have become so disheartened by "the system" that they have chosen to homeschool their children. Once regarded as limited to a subgroup of White middle-class Christian families (McDowell, Sanchez, & Jones, 2000), current statistics suggest that homeschooling has expanded to all socioeconomic levels and ethnic groups (Bielick, Chandler, & Broughman, 2001). Indeed, during the spring of 1999, an estimated 709,000 to 992,000 students were homeschooled. The most common reason parents gave for homeschooling is a belief that they can give the child a better education at home, as opposed to citing religious beliefs or convenience (Bielick et al.). Others take more drastic measures, such as the 40 Hmong (a Southeast Asian ethnic group) parents who threatened to take their children out of elementary school if the district did not address their concerns about the quality of their children's education (Matlosz, 2002).

Public dissatisfaction with special education is also apparent. When Public Law 94-142 was first passed in 1975, the emphasis was on the provision of education to children who had been denied access (Carnine & Granzin, 2001). More recently, greater attention has been given to the quality of outcomes for those students served under IDEA (Ysseldyke, Thurlow, Kozleski, & Reschly, 1998). Indeed, in 1993 a unanimous Supreme Court ruling (*Florence County School District Four v. Carter,* 1993) established that parents can obtain alternative or additional services, paid for by the district, if there is a failure to make progress toward goals identified in the individualized education plan (IEP). Many parents have either heard or been told horror stories of children who have failed to acquire even basic skills despite their "special" education. Other parents are reluctant to have their children enter the system for fear that they will be stuck and will not be granted a high school diploma. It should be noted that parents who "actively seek out and use services have higher expectations for the service system and thus are likely to be less satisfied than those who have lower expectations for assistance" (Bailey, Skinner, Rodriguez, Gut, & Correa, 1999, p. 378).

The elaborate special education referral process generates significant paperwork, much of which seems useless both to parents and teachers. Often, general education teachers do not have copies of IEP goals and objectives or do not feel the IEP is relevant to what happens in their classrooms (Menlove, Hudson, & Suter, 2001). One general education teacher admitted that in her first years of teaching, she "had no idea" what the IEP was and that she had little understanding of what the resource room teacher did with her student with special needs. It was not until the resource teacher admonished her for not getting the student to resource room on time that she began to pay closer attention to making accommodations for students with special needs. Another high school teacher stated that there were "too many IEPs to do an effective job of development and monitoring on" (Stowitschek, Lovitt, & Rodriguez, 2001, p. 109).

Some parents go through intense negotiation of their child's IEP, only to find their child still is not receiving the services listed on the IEP. For example, one mother felt she was being conciliatory when she relented on all of her requests except for speech therapy. Six months after the IEP was signed, her daughter still was not receiving services due to personnel problems. With a mound of signed papers in front of them, parents may ask what difference it all makes for their child.

Some insight into why so many parents have become disenchanted with the current educational system can be found in the ideological shift toward seeing parents as *citizen consumers.*

> While previous educational reform movements have focused on curriculum and teaching methods, today's reforms center on issues of governance.... A core belief underlying most current reform proposals is that education cannot be improved unless new actors are brought into the decision process ... shifting power toward parents, and exposing an overly bureaucratized system of education to some form of market discipline. (Schneider, Marschall, Teske, & Roch, 1998, pp. 489–490)

Rather than see themselves as peripheral, many of today's parents view themselves as having an integral role.

UNDERSTANDING DISSATISFACTION

In this culture of disenchantment, it may not take much for any individual parent to become dissatisfied with his or her child's education. At the crux of many parents' discontent is the belief that the school is solely responsible for their children's education. Historically, school professionals, including teachers, have been depicted as experts and parents as non-experts. Federal mandates for greater parental involvement (IDEA, 1997), however, are changing this notion. By requiring professionals to involve parents in the educational decision-making process, IDEA portrays parents as equal partners with educators (Turnbull & Turnbull, 1998).

While most parents would agree to being treated as equals, these same parents balk at sharing responsibility when problems occur. Instead, they tend to see educators as being in charge and their role as supplemental. In these instances, parents may become frustrated or disappointed that they need to be involved to keep the school accountable. However, as one guide to special education advised parents,

> If you buy a toaster that doesn't work as it's supposed to, you take action.... You don't wring your hands and wait for the company to find you. It's the same with IDEA.... The full implementation of the law depends on parents. (Cutler, 1993, p. 3)

Rather than share this view, most parents blame educators and schools for any shortcomings.

This may be particularly true among families of low socioeconomic status (SES). One study found that while high SES parents were able to customize their child's schooling by hiring outside help (e.g., a phonics tutor), low SES parents were not and expected the school to meet the child's needs (Coots, 1998). These parents were subsequently viewed as difficult parents, and their children continued to receive inadequate services.

Another issue is parents' expectations for public education. Many parents expect the system to provide for every child's individualized needs. However, federal law ensures a free, *appropriate* public education for all, not a free, *ideal* education for all. Recent court cases have affirmed this position. "Parents cannot be guaranteed their child will receive maximum educational opportunity; instead they must be satisfied with 'some educational benefit'" (Bhat, Rapport, & Griffin, 2000, p. 291). Nevertheless, parents expect the system to do what is best for their individual child, period, not to provide what they can given financial considerations and the like. One parent of a student with special needs stated,

> It can be very disappointing and a big letdown when you realize the limitations of the public school system. It's more disappointing than learning about the limitations of your child. When your child is diagnosed with special needs or whatever, you know, you go through a grief process. Well, you also go though a grief process when you realize the special education system has a disorder. (Lake & Billingsley, 2000, p. 247)

When parents of students with special needs are told their child needs more than the school can provide, they often feel betrayed by the school system. For example, the National Academy of Sciences (NAS) issued a report in 2001 recommending at least 24 hours per week of intensive behavioral intervention for children with autism. Unfortunately, fewer than 10% of autistic children receive it, in part because school districts are reluctant to pay for this particular expensive treatment (Gross, 2003). A parent who is aware of the NAS recommendation would understandably feel shortchanged if his or her child was not receiving optimal treatment.

Issues of cultural diversity also play a role in parents' expectations for public education and for teachers. Parents from different ethnic groups may have different expectations for their children's academic success. As a whole, immigrants tend to place a heavy emphasis on academic achievement (Siu, 1994). Though they are most likely to put pressure on their children for improving performance, they may also be disappointed in the teachers' lack of results. One immigrant Chinese parent lamented that the American school system was too lax and did not expect enough from students (Gorman, 1998). This sentiment was echoed by a Mexican father, who felt his son's teacher did not spend enough time teaching the basics.

Similarly, parents of low SES also want schools to provide their children with the opportunity to succeed in the greater society by equipping them with the necessary skills. Rather than valuing progressive or liberal education (e.g., character education, cooperative learning, open classrooms)

(Schneider et al., 1998), many low-income, inner-city parents want a more traditional academic curriculum (Delpit, 1995).

> These parents are more likely to value schools that perform the bedrock function of providing a safe environment in which the fundamentals of education are delivered . . . to increase the likelihood that their children can pass the "gatekeeping points" on the path to economic success. (Schneider et al., 1998)

As a result, they may not approve of more abstract or subjective ways of evaluating student performance, such as student portfolios, and may want to see tangible signs of success, such as high test scores (Schneider et al., 1998).

Other parents are disappointed by the types of services their students with special needs receive. Parents may feel their children require more services, such as additional sessions with the speech therapist or more assistive technology, than the school provides. Some parents may be discouraged by their child's lack of progress and request specific instructional methods or approaches, such as the Orton-Gillingham method for teaching reading (Bhat et al., 2000). Still other parents are not initially aware of their options in education. For example, in studies of culturally diverse families, parents readily agreed to have their children with disabilities placed in segregated settings, primarily because they did not know they had a choice (Harry, 1998; Harry, Kalyanpur, & Day, 1999). Becoming aware of their rights after the fact may lead some to become dissatisfied with programs they initially readily agreed to.

RESPONDING WHEN PARENTS REJECT THE INDIVIDUAL EDUCATION PLAN (IEP)

Typically, when school professionals convene to plan a student's IEP, a great deal of thought is put into the elements of the plan. In contrast, in many schools, parents view their participation in IEP planning meetings as token or superficial. As one mother said, "They have it all written out and put together already. What else am I supposed to say?" As a result, they may not give input, or even attend the meetings, knowing that the papers will be mailed to them to sign.

In these schools, teachers who are accustomed to acquiescence by parents may be annoyed by relentless parents who are actively engaged in planning their child's IEP. These parents may express great dissatisfaction with certain elements of the IEP or with the entire plan. For example, some parents may want their child mainstreamed and resist services that do not support that goal. Others may be troubled by a lack of specificity in goals and services. One mother lamented that there were no written objectives for physical education and was told, "We'll work that out when the school year starts." Another fumed that her son's IEP stated as an objective, "Regular gym as the schedule allows" (Cutler, 1993). Although the school may genuinely intend to address these specifics, the parent cannot be assured of this. One book for parents of students with special needs cautioned,

> Remember that talk is cheap . . . and when you go back after a few months to check on the implementation of the IEP, you will be able to advocate for only what is written in the program. . . . And without written agreements you will probably hear about the tight budget and shortage of personnel that does not allow for more service for your child. (Cutler, p. 162)

When confronted with this type of dissatisfaction, try not to take the parents' complaints personally. Parents who consistently advocate for specific services for their children are clearly invested in the process and the product, and this should be encouraged rather than discouraged. While the parents may trust you to have their child's best interests at heart, they know that the IEP is not an agreement between you and them, but a legal contract with the school system that stays effective regardless of the environment, such as a change of personnel or schools.

For some parents, rejecting the IEP is their only means of expressing their dissatisfaction with how their child is progressing in school. They may feel desperate, ignored, or misunderstood by the school and may use rejection of the IEP as a sign to all that they are serious. Whether the rejection is consciously calculated or an act of frustration, it does not necessarily mean that parents are unwilling to discuss and negotiate further. When you lease a car, you may object to the terms of the lease (e.g., the cost of extra mileage), but that does not mean that you do not want the car or that you object to the salesperson. Similarly, parents who reject an IEP are dissatisfied with the contract, not necessarily with you or other educators, or with your educational judgment. Applaud these parents for their tenacity and love for their children. Parents who reject an IEP can still be encouraged to talk over areas of disagreement and to informally resolve their concerns without resorting to a hearing or litigation.

COPING WITH THE CONSEQUENCES OF DISSATISFACTION

Parents' dissatisfaction may lead them, at the minimum, to question your teaching practices and, at the extreme, to seek alternate placement for their child. Parents may become manipulative, seeking to obtain for their child what the school has failed to provide. For example, one mother felt her son's writing disability was not being sufficiently addressed and repeatedly requested that the school district provide a laptop computer for her son. When conventional avenues failed to achieve this, she had her son evaluated by a private psychologist, making it clear that she wanted the psychologist to document his need for the computer. She then presented the psychologist's 17-page report to the school, complete with recommendations for a laptop. The school did not comply, in large part because the recommendation for a laptop was handwritten at the end of the report—by the mother. Another couple seized upon a minor error made by their son's teacher and threatened to sue the district. In the end, their son was granted a host of services, including a one-to-one paraprofessional.

Other parents may grasp onto a specific program or service that was beneficial for another child and demand that the school provide it for their child. For example, the parents of a sixth grader with a learning disability repeatedly requested a specific computer program for their son, despite the school's insistence that other approaches (e.g., small group instruction) would be more effective. These parents had heard about the success of the computer program from their advocate, whose daughter had used it. Parents who feel the school is not providing appropriate solutions will find their own. They often hold to their ideas even when other good alternatives are put forth, simply because they no longer trust the school's judgment.

Still other parents may go through the IEP process, only to unilaterally place their child in a private school. For example, one father stated, "My daughter's kindergarten experience was a disaster. Anything that could go wrong did. She felt stigmatized and so did we. After that year, we put her into a private school. She is much happier" (Bernard, 2001, p. 202).

In some cases, such as when children were performing three or more years below grade level, hearing officers and judges have ruled in favor of the parents, ordering school districts to reimburse parents for expenses incurred from private school placement (e.g., tuition) (Bhat et al., 2000).

Although most parents do not litigate when dissatisfied, their displeasure is nonetheless clear. Parents may feel that the teacher's ineptitude was responsible for their child's problems. For example, one parent was upset that her son received a midyear grade of B and demanded to know why. When the teacher explained that the student's two-week absence for a family trip resulted in missed work, the parent blamed the teacher for not supplying all the work that the student needed to do in advance of the trip. Another parent of a boy with dyslexia commented, "My son didn't learn anything last year; his teacher was really terrible." Disgruntled parents often make teachers feel inadequate, sometimes purposefully, sometimes not.

While there may be a grain of truth in parents' accusations, usually teachers are not completely to blame. As a result, you may feel offended by dissatisfied parents, because you are doing everything you can to be a good teacher, devoting time and energy above and beyond the call of duty.

This is especially true if you hear about the parents' dissatisfaction from someone other than the parent. Remember that although you may feel hurt, the most severe consequences are felt by someone else. As Adele Unterberg, an educator with 34 years of experience, asserts, "There are parents who only come to school to argue and find fault. They blame everyone—especially the teachers—for countless problems. The *child* is the one who suffers in the end."

HANDLING MEDIATION AND DUE PROCESS HEARINGS

When students first enter the special education system, parents are informed that they have the right to due process any time they disagree with the educational agency about their child's assessment, program, or placement (Hogan, 1990). Two options for due process are the prehearing conference (PHC) and an impartial due process hearing. Parents may initiate due process hearings if they feel their concerns are not being sufficiently addressed and the PHC was unsuccessful in resolving the dispute (or they waived their right to a PHC). The costs of these legal proceedings are high, not only financially but emotionally taxing as well. In one case, a due process hearing for a Pennsylvania child required 19 sessions over a 2-year period (Zirkel, 1994). The cost of the hearing officer alone was $20,000; expenses for the attorneys, court transcripts, and staff time were similarly exorbitant. While objections to placements are the most common reasons for seeking due process hearings (Smith, 1981), other issues, such as the child's classification, eligibility, procedural issues, and the content and implementation of the IEP, may result in hearings (Fielding, 1990; U.S. General Accounting Office, 1989).

These hearings take place before an impartial hearing officer, who renders a decision after hearing evidence and cross-examination from the parents and the school. Because of the adversarial nature of hearings, parents and teachers often find themselves depicted as enemies, where each side highlights the other's errors. Although it is not a substitute for a due process hearing, mediation can be more effective, since it tends to focus on communication and cooperation by allowing parents and schools to reach an accord together (Fielding, 1990). Because solutions are not imposed by a hearing officer, it is probable that both parents and teachers will be more vested in a successful outcome (Hogan, 1990). In addition, mediation is less costly than due process hearings and less threatening, but at the same time, highly successful. As a result, it is more accessible to all parents, not just wealthy ones who can afford an attorney. Although IDEA (1997) identifies voluntary mediation as a means of resolving parent–school disputes (Lytle & Bordin, 2001), not all state departments of education offer mediation. However, such services can be found in the private sector in all states.

Table 4.1 Main Principles for Dealing With Dissatisfaction
Principle 1: Focus on the Problem, Not the Person
Principle 2: Ask for Parents' Solutions
Principle 3: Stay Focused on the End Goal

If informal meetings and an IEP review have been unsuccessful in resolving parents' dissatisfaction, teachers can encourage disgruntled parents to use mediation services. Mediation is appropriate even if the parents plan to pursue a due process hearing, since mediation does not delay or deny due process rights (Hogan, 1990). Making such a suggestion is not an admission of wrongdoing, a betrayal of the school system, or an inappropriate overstepping of professional boundaries. Rather, informing parents of the benefits of mediation reinforces your role as a collaborator. It conveys your desire to talk and work things out and reluctance to take the matter to court. At the end of mediation proceedings, you and the parents will have a signed written agreement from which to work together for the student's benefit. Perhaps most important, this agreement will reflect decisions made by the people who know the child the best—you and the parents—rather than others (i.e., judges and attorneys) who are quite removed from the child (Bhat et al., 2000).

MAIN PRINCIPLES FOR DEALING WITH DISSATISFACTION

Ideally, resolving conflicts with dissatisfied parents would occur through informal channels, rather than having to resort to mediation and due process proceedings. The following principles should guide you when dealing with discontented parents.

Principle 1: Focus on the Problem, Not the Person

When meeting with dissatisfied parents, it is easy to become distracted by their negativity, especially if they are blaming you for the problem. Keep your emotions in check and try not to take the parents' complaints personally. This enables you to think rationally about how to address the problem effectively. Seasoned negotiators Fisher, Ury, and Patton (1991) suggest that keeping the attention on the problem (and not the person) allows the parent to save face. Why is saving face important? Because people tend to become more entrenched in their positions if backed into a corner. If you tell a parent, "You really shouldn't be so critical. Your child is getting the best education in the district," you are setting the parent up to defend their disappointment.

Take time to get as much information as you can about what the problem is. If a parent protests that his or her son is not communicating as well as he should, ask for details and elicit examples. Clarify any statements that may be unclear. For example, the complaint, "he can't follow directions," may mean different things to you and to the parent. Getting detailed information helps you identify a specific problem, which makes it more likely that you will be able to do something about it. It also changes the dynamics of your interactions with the dissatisfied parent. Rather than being a complainer and a defensive target, you and the parent become collaborators, identifying a problem and its solutions. In addition, focusing on the problem (and not the person) helps the parent to do the same. "If you want [the parent] to listen to you, begin by listening to him. If you want him to acknowledge your point, acknowledge his first" (Ury, 1991, p. 37).

Principle 2: Ask for Parents' Solutions

Dissatisfied parents are often quite good at telling you what the problem is, but are not as able to articulate what the solution might be. Getting parents to think about what they see as possible solutions for the problem not only changes their mindset from complaining to collaborating, it may also produce an actual solution. If parents do offer a solution, be respectful of it, rather than telling them why it is not feasible. William Ury, internationally known negotiator and mediation expert, states,

> If parents do offer a solution, be respectful of it, rather than telling them why it is not feasible.

> Once you have elicited your opponent's ideas, you need to build on them. This doesn't mean accepting them as they are. Rather, select the ideas you find most constructive, and starting with them, head off in the direction you want to go. . . . Building on his ideas does not mean shortchanging your own. It means building a bridge from his thinking back to yours. (Ury, 1991, p. 93)

Ury (1991) also suggests asking, "What would you suggest that I do?" or "What would you do if you were in my shoes?" as a way to engage the parent in a discussion of options. He explains that asking "your opponent" for advice "not only disarms him, but also gives you a chance to educate him about your problem and the constraints facing you" (p. 67).

If the parent gives you an idea, pick apart its merits. For example, if the parent requests a computer program, you may acknowledge the benefits of immediate feedback, self-guided instruction, or other elements that may be part of a solution.

Principle 3: Stay Focused on the End Goal

Similarly, keep your (and their) focus on the ultimate aim and try to avoid being mired in many side issues. For example, a mother may complain that her child is not getting enough individual attention and, as a result, is not making progress in math. Rather than discuss all the various ways you (and other teachers) provide individual attention and explain reasons why you cannot do more, put the focus on the mother's desire to see her child's math skills improve. Does the mother want to see higher test scores, reduced reliance on a calculator, improved problem solving, decreased math anxiety, or other indications that her child's math is making progress? By honing on the desired product and minimizing discussion of the process (i.e., responding to each of the parent's litany of complaints), you can identify steps to take to reduce the parent's dissatisfaction.

OTHER STRATEGIES FOR DEALING WITH DISSATISFACTION

Anne Wescott Dodd, author of *A Parent's Guide to Innovative Education* (1992) and education chair at Bates College, makes three recommendations in her guidebook (1998) for teachers:

> First, because parents make judgments about school programmes and practices based on their children's experiences, they need good information about what is actually going on. . . . Second, when parents are concerned or critical, educators should take time to discuss the problem in some depth with parents because it is easy to misunderstand their critical comments. . . . Third, when educators plan changes in school programmes or classroom practices, parents need to be involved from the beginning. (Dodd, 1998, p. 475)

She also suggests that educators recruit parents for focus groups when changes in school programming are initially considered. Increasing parental involvement in general also has the potential to provide parents with firsthand information on what is positive in the classroom (e.g., the merits of a particular writing method) and may reduce parents' yearnings for "something else" (Bhat et al., 2000).

In addition, it is important to remember that when one parent makes a complaint, it is safe to assume that there is at least one other parent that feels similarly, though that parent may or may not voice the concern. Treat each complaint seriously. A parent may have a laundry list of complaints, but may be choosing to only voice one. As one parent explained,

> When I finished tearing out my hair, I decided that we parents must pick our fights. I was reluctant to undermine my daughter's relationship with her teacher and wary that the teacher, resenting my efforts, might take it out on my daughter, if only unconsciously. (Cohen, 2002, p. F1)

Thus, other complaints may have been brewing; be aware that you may have only seen the tip of the iceberg.

Last, Leslie Amani, a sixth-grade teacher in Los Banos, California, stresses the importance of being professional and positive. She recounted an experience in which parents who had enlisted an advocate to help fight their cause eventually changed their adversarial stance and actually approached her for guidance. She states she was always careful in her speech, using phrases like "It seems like . . ." and "It appears . . ." when communicating sensitive information and that she shared positive information about the child's reading with the parents. She reflects, "I don't think I did anything special. I think they finally felt like they were listened to."

WORKING WITH ADVOCATES

Many teachers feel intimidated by the presence of a law advocate. Advocates are hired by parents who feel they need to bolster their case, perhaps because their prior attempts to resolve disagreements were unsuccessful. Advocates may be other parents who have developed advocacy skills from dealing with their own children with special needs or professionals specially trained for advocacy in education. Some may be congenial and play the role of the supportive friend. Others may be quite adversarial and treat school staff as defendants on trial.

Whatever the case, do not be intimidated by advocates. Remember that they were invited by the parents and treat them with respect, not avoidance or wariness. Most likely, their expertise in the fine points of the special education system and education laws will exceed yours. It is in the best interests of all involved—school, parents, and child—that legal obligations are met and appropriate services are provided. Recognize this and treat advocates as equal partners in the process of trying to provide what is best for the child. In so doing, you remove the intimidation factor of having an outsider who is an expert, and the advocate becomes just another team member.

Direct your statements and inquiries to the parents rather than treating the advocate as their spokesperson. Advocates should empower the parents they work with, not treat them as victims needing to be rescued. If an antagonistic advocate is taking this infantilizing approach, it is appropriate to openly recognize it. You can say, "I appreciate your expertise. I'm sure Mr. and Mrs. So-and-so also have something to say."

WHAT TO AVOID

When dealing with parents who are dissatisfied with their child's education, there are two types of responses that are generally inappropriate. The first type is responses that are rejecting or insensitive. Particularly with parents who make frequent demands, you may be tempted to dismiss their complaints and dissatisfaction as unrealistic or as yet another demand. Perhaps it is true that they have impractical ideas, but telling them so will do little except raise their anger. Other insensitive responses are statements that communicate an unwillingness to help, such as "I can't do anything about it. It's school policy." These types of responses tend to make dissatisfied parents even more disappointed and frustrated.

The second type of inappropriate response is a reply that creates false hopes or leads parents on rather than saying no, even when you know there is virtually no chance their request will be granted. Most of us will try to avoid an angry parent's wrath and do not want to be the party pooper. Although saying yes when you mean no will provide you with relief in the *immediate* situation, it is likely to make things worse for the school professional who eventually does say no, since disappointment is more intense when hopes are high.

Consider the following scenario. The parents of a student with Down's syndrome corner you after school and state, "Sydney hasn't made much progress in communicating, and we think it's because she isn't getting enough services. Our friend's son was just given his own computer and a software program called Exploratory Play by the school district and it's really made a difference. We think Sydney needs the same thing too."

One issue to deal with is your emotional reaction to being told that one of your students has not made progress under your care. Do not respond in anger or defensiveness, and try to clarify their perceptions of the lack of progress so you can discuss that issue instead of the request for additional assistive technology. Next you may be tempted to deal with their dissatisfaction in the following two inappropriate ways. A *rejecting response* would be "Those computer language programs are only for kids with severe disabilities, and Sydney doesn't need it." The parents obviously feel she does need it, and stating that you do not agree, without discussing the reasons behind their feelings, cuts off the communication and raises the parents' discontent. The *false hopes response* would be to say, "That's an interesting idea. I think you should talk to the special education director about it." Rather than state outright that you do not think it is appropriate because Sydney is already receiving adequate services, you pass it off to another person. After the parents go through multiple channels, talking to various professionals about their desire for the computer and software, they may resent being given the runaround, especially if, in the end, they are told that it is unnecessary because you (and others) feel she is making adequate progress.

Being upfront and realistic in the beginning is a better approach, such as saying, "If Sydney really needs a computer and special software to reach her IEP goals, she may be able to get them. But what makes you think she isn't making progress? I think she has really improved in her vocabulary and comprehension."

GOING BEYOND DISSATISFACTION

Researchers have identified two types of disappointment (van Dijk & Zeelenberg, 2002). Outcome-related disappointment occurs when the results do not match up to the expectations, such as failing an exam. In these situations, the person tends to feel sad, to want a second chance, and to try harder. In contrast, person-related disappointment occurs when an individual is to blame for an undesirable situation, such as when a friend spreads rumors about you. In these situations, the person tends to be angry and to ignore or avoid the other individual.

If the parents you are working with are upset because of an undesirable outcome, such as a second-choice placement for their child, you can help them overcome their sadness by encouraging them to make other efforts to achieve what they desire. This may mean providing resources for supports outside of the school or helping parents think and plan for next year's placement issues. Reinforcing their hope for a better outcome next time is helpful for getting parents to move past their disappointment.

If the parents are experiencing disappointment related to an individual (or to school professionals in general), focus instead on rebuilding trust. Perhaps the parents feel you or the school misled or deceived them or did not value their input despite asking for it. Whatever responsibility you hold for the situation—a little or a great deal—take steps to make amends. Apologize, be conscientious about addressing their concerns, and openly acknowledge the need to reestablish a trusting relationship with them. Even if you bear no responsibility for their dissatisfaction, you may need to rebuild trust because parents see you as part of the system.

Not all parents' desires for their children can be fulfilled, and helping parents cope with disappointment in their children's schooling is an important part of establishing realistic expectations for their children and for you. If parents are dissatisfied with the current state of affairs, encourage them to use their talents and clout to change what they are complaining about. Making the best of what is available and finding creative ways to work within the system are essential skills for parents in their roles as advocates for student with special needs.

REFLECTING ON YOUR TEACHING

Many teachers encounter dissatisfied parents and many do not know how to address parental dissatisfaction beyond being sympathetic. Use the following questions and activities to reflect on your own approaches and to guide you in working with disgruntled parents.

1. How do you tend to handle your own disappointments or dissatisfaction (e.g., take action, expect someone else to fix it)? How does this impact your expectations of parents who are dissatisfied?

2. To what extent do you feel responsible for and capable of addressing parents' dissatisfaction? Do you feel it is the responsibility of school administrators rather than teachers?

3. To what extent are you able to separate your own emotions and personality conflicts from the problems identified by dissatisfied parents (e.g., do you tend to feel defensive)?

4. Imagine how you would handle a situation in which a parent threatens to sue or pursue an impartial hearing.

5. When was the last time you asked for and chose to implement a parent's solution to a problem you identified?

SUMMARY

The real inadequacies of schools and parents' expectations for public (and in particular, special) education contribute to current dissatisfaction with public education. The school's values may also conflict with those of ethnic minority groups and families of low socioeconomic status. In addition, an ideological shift toward parents as consumers leads parents to be disappointed when they do not receive what they feel entitled to. Applying the mediation principles of focusing on the problem (not the person), asking parents to identify solutions, and staying focused on the end goal is helpful for dealing with parents who are disappointed. In addition, it may be necessary to reestablish trust if parents believe school professionals are responsible for the negative outcome. Avoid *rejecting responses* and those that give parents *false hope*, both of which tend to fuel dissatisfaction. Parents who reject an IEP or enlist a law advocate are examples of individuals whose disappointment can be a hindrance or a catalyst. Motivating parents to continue to work within the system and have realistic expectations for their child and school is paramount to supporting parents' roles as advocates for their child.

DEALING WITH NONPARTICIPATION AND RESISTANCE

"After seven (!) failed appointments for which she had various excuses, the stepmother refused to talk to the School Based Support Team at all."

Vera Kishinevsky, Ph.D.
School Psychologist
15 years of teaching experience
Bronx, NY

Y ou prepare for days for Back-to-School Night, only to have a total of three parents come. You have concerns about a student but are repeatedly unsuccessful in your efforts to meet with the parents. You think a specific placement will help a student but cannot get the parents to agree to it. These situations are frustrating and, unfortunately, fairly common. This chapter discusses parents' nonparticipation in general as well as ways to handle parents who fail to come to appointments or who resist your interventions.

SHARING TEACHERS' VIEWS

At the risk of oversimplification, teachers tend to fall into three camps. One group of teachers think that lack of parent participation in their children's education is problematic. For example, a sixth-grade teacher lamented, "I can deal with the parents who yell and are pushy. It's the ones that don't care—who don't care at all—that really get to me." Other teachers see parent nonparticipation as a blessing of sorts. As one teacher put it, "My school doesn't have a lot of parent involvement, so thankfully I don't have to deal with them much." Still others are focused on educating their students and have not given parent involvement much thought. Though they interact with parents as necessary, such as during mandatory parent–teacher conferences, they are not consciously looking for ways to integrate parents in their teaching. Jeana Preston, head of San Diego City Schools' parent-involvement program, reflected on her preparation for teaching: "Nobody ever mentioned to me that kids had parents. . . . Imagine my shock upon finding that there were parents" (Jones, 2001, p. 20).

All three opinions are understandable. It is beneficial for parents to be involved in their children's education, as evidenced by research linking parental involvement with gains in reading, positive attitudes about school, and better homework habits (Hewison, 1988; Epstein, 2000). At the same time, parent involvement creates more work for teachers, at least initially, causing some to avoid it. Hancock (1998) notes that "parent involvement is actually a very demanding form of curriculum development for a class teacher," which may require "a number of additional professional skills for which no training was given" (p. 410). Also, with curricular demands and student concerns, it is easy for some teachers to overlook the component of parent involvement.

DISCERNING NONINVOLVEMENT VERSUS NONPARTICIPATION

It is important to note that nonparticipation does not necessarily mean noninvolvement. For example, many teachers view minority parents and parents with low socioeconomic status as indifferent and uninvolved in their children's education (Davies, 1993). In reality, many of these parents value education as a means of social mobility (Lopez, 2002) and have a genuine interest in their child's education (Trueba & Delgado-Gaitan, 1988). These parents are involved in their children's education, yet they never set foot in the classroom or initiate contact with the teacher.

For instance, there is generally minimal Chinese American parent presence in schools as volunteers, advocates for their children, or participants in policy making (Siu, 1994). Yet, among many immigrant Chinese families, parents structure family life around and sacrifice a great deal for their children's education. They may excuse their children from household chores so that they can devote more time to studying, provide tutors, or provide unlimited financial resources for educational tools (Gorman, 1998). However, these immigrant parents may feel uncomfortable taking a more open role in their children's studies, such as by volunteering in the classroom. In part, this may be due to parents' concerns over their English language proficiency (Gorman).

Similarly, Latino parents may feel they are involved in their children's education even if they do not attend meetings at school. In one study, Latino parents defined their educational roles and responsibilities primarily as

(a) Ensuring their child's attendance
(b) Instilling respect for the teacher
(c) Encouraging and expecting good behavior in school by their child
(d) Meeting their obligations to provide clothing, shelter, and food for their children (sometimes in the face of considerable poverty)
(e) Socializing their child to their family responsibilities

Source: Chrispeels & Rivero (2001, p. 160).

Many teachers would see this as insufficient, because responsibilities such as helping with homework and communicating with the teacher are absent.

In these types of situations, open discussion of what teachers and schools expect from parents can correct misunderstandings about non-involvement. For example, in Chrispeel and Rivero's (2001) research, Latino parents attended classes at schools focusing on topics such as how the school system works, academic standards, and home–school collaboration. "A major discovery by parents was that they could initiate contact with the school and did not have to wait for the teacher to extend an invitation" (Christpeel & Rivero, p. 161). Be careful not to assume that a parent who fails to come to an appointment or does not volunteer in the classroom is not involved in the child's education. Rather, there may be valid reasons—cultural or otherwise—that impede their participation.

UNDERSTANDING NONPARTICIPATION

Again at the risk of oversimplification, nonparticipatory parents seem to fall into three camps. Some parents' overall lack of involvement and interest in their children's education may be a reflection of their own negative experiences with school. Education does not seem to be essential or even relevant to their children's futures, because these parents did not experience their schooling as helpful in their own lives. They may or may not have graduated from high school to get uninteresting jobs that require little skill and offer no room for advancement. Perhaps the parents' own experience of school was drudgery, and they were happy to have that part of their lives over with. These parents view their children's education as something they have to do but that is quite useless. They may view other nonacademic skills as more useful in the long run and may not value time spent on learning history and creative writing skills. For example, in some rural communities, hard physical labor may be seen as more valuable than sitting behind a desk (Bauch, 2001). These parents may hesitate to respond when their participation is requested. Some parents may be intimidated by teachers and school officials, who are viewed as authority figures (McEwan, 1998). They may resist invitations to become more involved or volunteer in the classroom and may resent being treated as if they are the teacher's employees or aides. Furthermore, they may loathe "being told how to work in teacherly ways with their children" (Edwards & Warin, 1999, p. 333).

> Some parents' overall lack of involvement and interest in their children's education may be a reflection of their own negative experiences with school.

Other parents do care but for various reasons are not able to be involved in their children's education as they would like. It is estimated that 80% of inmates are parents of dependent children. Though they may desire involvement, they clearly are restricted in their ability to participate (Barry, 1995). Many parents have demanding jobs that significantly limit the amount of time they have for their families. One teacher in a rural community stated that 90% of her students had parents who worked "over the hill," requiring a daily commute of 1 to 2 hours each way. Another father stated that although he wished he could attend school functions as other parents did, he could not, because he worked both a day job and a night job in order to provide for his family of seven.

Some parents may be overwhelmed with other needs of their families. One father was overwhelmed trying to care for his two children—a fourth grader with special needs and a newborn daughter born with hydrocephaly—and deal with his schizophrenic wife. He lamented, "One minute my wife is telling me I have a basketball on my head and now the school is calling me about Jade not paying attention in class." Another mother explained her failure to follow through on the team's recommendation for karate lessons for their son, who has motor coordination problems:

> It is hard to know what is essential and when it's okay to say, "enough." You've got all these professionals who recommend all these things, and they all believe in those things and see them as important. But we have two other kids. What about their needs?

These parents may seem resistant to your recommendations, yet they are simply trying their best to balance the many responsibilities they have.

Still others are not aware of the need for parent involvement. These parents may love their children but may be unsure of what is best for them in an educational sense. They may not know enough to be able to comment on the merits of one placement over another or may lack information on developmentally appropriate expectations for their child. For example, you may find that parent participation drops off in the latter grades. Parents who may have been involved when their children were just starting school may think that their involvement is not needed when their child is older. One sixth-grade teacher stated, "I have to practically beg for chaperones on field trips." In addition, parents may view teacher entreaties to be more active in their children's education, both at home and in the classroom, as superficial or obligatory rather than genuine. It may be helpful to remind these parents of the importance of continued involvement, such as by sending a letter suggesting ways to be involved. A sample letter for parents of older elementary students can be found in Resource C.

Also, parents differ in how they interpret the same events. Some people see a doctor for a cold; others wait until their broken bone is protruding. Similarly, if a parent is told, "Your child is having a problem paying attention," some will see it as needing immediate action, while others will see it as fine to wait and see if the problem resolves itself. Some parents, because of their cultural background or beliefs about disability (Danesco, 1997), may see education as the role domain of experts such as teachers. These parents may be unaware that they can intervene in their children's education as well. As a result, they may not offer input, even when solicited, or question professionals' recommendations (Kalyanpur & Rao, 1991).

UNDERSTANDING NONPARTICIPATION OF PARENTS OF ADOLESCENTS

A high school English teacher stated that one year she had 15 students with special needs, yet did not have a single encounter with their parents.

Although she attributed this to "the way high schools work in general," many reasons account for reduced parent participation at the secondary school level. Adolescents may discourage their parents from being visibly involved at school (e.g., volunteering at school), and overall communication with parents may lessen. Parents of adolescents may not know ways they can be involved once their children reach high school. Parents of students with special needs may be discouraged from actively intervening by their lack of success in producing positive results. Specifically, parents may feel they do not make much of a difference in their adolescent's achievement-related outcomes and consequently decide to get involved less frequently at the secondary level (Deslandes, Royer, Potvin, & LeClerc, 1999). All of these factors contribute to parents' general nonparticipation once their children reach high school.

However, a growing body of evidence suggests that parental involvement at the secondary school level is just as important. Parental involvement has been found to be associated with higher student attendance, better behavior, and increased time and effort on homework (Deslandes et al., 1999; Lee, 1994); higher aspirations (Trusty, 1996); and academic achievement (Steinberg, Lamborn, Dornbusch, & Darling, 1992), as well as reduced delinquency, pregnancies, and dropout rates (Wang, Haertel, & Walberberg, 1993/1994).

Bear in mind that involvement at the middle and secondary levels differs from parental involvement in the elementary level and rightly so. Different types of involvement are effective at different times during the student's life (Muller, 1993). Parents of adolescents need to respect their growing autonomy, and adolescents may resist certain forms of parental involvement (Epstein & Connors, 1995). Nonetheless, most adolescents want their parents to be involved in their schooling, especially if it is private and does not involve peers or teachers (Deslandes & Cloutier, 2002).

 Parents of adolescents need to be encouraged to continue providing affective support (e.g., talking with their children about the importance of hard work and time management), which may be more effective in impacting student achievement and behavior than direct support strategies such as talking with the teacher or visiting the classroom (McNeal, 1999). Furthermore, parental aspirations for their children's education have also been found to be related to school achievement and should be encouraged (Singh et al., 1995). In addition, parents need to be informed of the importance of monitoring their adolescents' friendships and activities, which has been found to exert a significant impact on their achievement. Monitoring enables parents to detect problems and take action before they become serious (Falbo, Lein, & Amador, 2001). A sample letter directed at parents of adolescents is presented in Resource D.

BEING SENSITIVE TO CONCERNS OF CULTURALLY AND LINGUISTICALLY DIVERSE PARENTS

Studies of culturally and linguistically diverse groups have found many reasons why their participation in schools is limited. Some parents sense misinterpretation of their children's needs and may feel alienated. As a result, they withdraw their participation (Geenen, Powers, & Lopez-Vasquez, 2001). Others, such as Puerto Rican parents, may find it difficult to openly disagree with teachers or otherwise engage in a conflict with professionals because of a culturally based deference toward teachers (Harry, 1992a). Still other Hispanics may feel too embarrassed to speak directly to the teacher (Valdés, 1996). Many Hispanic migrant parents may not attend meetings because "they have very limited communication skills or feel they won't make a difference if they complain. Some even fear that if they complain, the teachers and the system will retaliate by suspending their children" (Leon, 1996, p. 10). The problem of mistrust among culturally and linguistically diverse parents is discussed further in Chapter 6.

In addition, research on parent involvement among culturally and linguistically diverse parents suggests that traditional forms of involvement may not be as effective. Specifically, being involved in parent–teacher organizations has been found to be associated with positive student outcomes for Caucasians and African Americans but not Hispanics or Asians. Also, parent–child discussion significantly reduces the likelihood of truancy and dropping out for Caucasians but not for African Americans, Hispanics, or Asians (McNeal, 1999). Thus, schools may be pressuring parents to engage in practices that are not culturally consistent or effective. It is not surprising then when culturally and linguistically diverse parents fail to follow through on these types of recommendations for parent involvement.

MAIN PRINCIPLES FOR DEALING WITH NONPARTICIPATION AND RESISTANCE

These four guiding principles will help you reach the majority of non-participatory parents. They work best when you are proactive, rather than waiting until the parents' lack of cooperation becomes infuriating.

Principle 1: Get to Know the Parents

By getting to know the parents, you can motivate them to be more involved and can gain cooperation by focusing on what is important to them. In one case, parents were very resistant to the school's suggestion

Table 5.1	Main Principles for Dealing With Nonparticipation and Resistance
Principle 1: Get to Know the Parents	
Principle 2: Be Creative	
Principle 3: Confront (Listen)	
Principle 4: Help Parents Participate	

that they try medication for their son with ADHD and rightfully so. Schools should not make pharmaceutical recommendations for medical diagnoses such as ADHD. Offended by this inappropriate suggestion, these parents were not persuaded by any discussion of the child's academic or social needs. Only after being persuaded that their child might be happier if his situation changed were they willing to consider discussing medication with their family physician. Sure enough, the son's mood was much more positive, and that convinced the parents that the school's other recommendations might have merit as well.

 True, it is hard to get to know parents whom you never see, but it is not impossible. If you cannot talk with them directly, talk with your students and other colleagues who have had contact with them to try to get to know what is important to the parents who do not participate as you would like. For example, the parents may be recent immigrants who are working two or more jobs just to meet their financial obligations. You may discern that education is very important to the parents, but they are unfamiliar with the American education system and its expectation for parent involvement. Alternatively, you may learn that the parents are intimidated by all the professionals involved with their children's education and that they feel they personally have nothing more to offer.

Other parents may need to interact with you in a nonthreatening nonacademic manner before feeling comfortable to participate in more complicated roles. For example, parents can be invited to visit the classroom as an observer or to be a presenter in the classroom on almost any topic—their career, their home country, their pets, and so forth. Interacting with them in this favorable manner will help set the stage for more complicated matters.

> Getting to know parents on a personal level is perhaps the best way to ward off nonparticipation.

Getting to know parents on a personal level is perhaps the best way to ward off nonparticipation. If parents do not have a relationship with the teacher, they are not bothered by not showing up. "People hardly ever miss their haircuts . . . they take that more seriously" (Jacob, 2002).

Principle 2: Be Creative

If the standard attempts at gaining parent cooperation have failed, get creative. When a parent has repeatedly failed to respond to notes sent home, for example, you might consider e-mailing them. There are many ways to utilize electronic communication. For example, you could encourage your students to become pen pals with their parents via e-mail, with regular correspondence detailing their work in the classroom. A class project to work on computer skills could be to send personalized invitations to conferences or requests to come see work in progress. Electronic communication has the benefits of building students' computer skills, making parents more aware of students' learning, and making parents more active in their children's literacy growth (Tao & Boulware, 2002).

Certainly, not all parents have access to e-mail. You can also engage parents by involving the student in other ways, while being careful not to put the responsibility on the student for the parent's cooperation. One second-grade teacher was frustrated that almost all of her weekly progress reports were unsigned and unreturned. She started putting a positive comment on each one (even the student who had only completed one of the week's assignments) and began reading them to each student in a 1-minute conference, where she reminded the student to have the parent sign the report. She was surprised when 75% of the reports were returned the next week. Clearly, the students were motivated to show the parents the notes, and the parents responded positively as well.

Yale University professor and child psychiatrist James Comer, whose schools have had much success in lower-SES communities, has a "proven recipe for bringing parents into schools: Feed them and put their kids on stage" (Jones, 2001, p. 21). Alternatively, you might try linking a student event with a parent conference that has been repeatedly missed, such as by arranging for a meeting with the parent after the school assembly. You can also try inviting a few parents to a Parent Appreciation Tea (put on by your students just before lunch) and asking the nonparticipatory parent to stay a few minutes to talk during lunch.

If your school does not offer parent educational activities, you might consider doing something simple on your own, such as a Read With Your Child workshop. Invite selected parents to visit your class during story time, so they can see you interact positively with their children and so they can learn some skills. (All the better if your targeted student chooses the book to be read and can invite his or her parents.) If you are seen as wanting to help them, they may want to help you in return.

Also, you can try mailing a letter explaining the benefits of parental involvement, such as those in Resources C and D, and then following up soon after with a specific request (e.g., to engage in interactive homework or attend a meeting). This one–two punch may propel the parent into action.

Principle 3: Confront (Listen)

A mother repeatedly fails to show up for appointments. Each time, she has some reason to explain her absence—the car broke down, she forgot, the baby was sick, and so forth. Rather than continue to make appointments and have the mother not show up, it may be appropriate to confront her on her resistance. Confronting in this sense should never be done in an accusatory manner. Rather, the point of the confrontation should be to ascertain if there is an underlying reason for the mother's absence—in actuality, this type of confrontation really means getting to the heart of the matter and listening to the parent. For example, you might say, "It's been really hard for you to come to the appointments, and I know you've had a lot going on (a lot of car trouble, etc.). But I'm also wondering if you have some concerns that haven't been addressed yet." You may even add, "In the past, when this has happened, it's been because the parents had some concerns that they hadn't voiced yet." Indeed, research has found that, for some parents, withholding or reducing participation has been used as a way to demonstrate disapproval (Harry, 1992b). The parent may or may not tell you what the concerns are, but at least you gave them the opportunity to tell you.

Some parents may fail to show up for meetings or participate when asked because they feel the requests are for token participation, such as putting their rubber stamp on an IEP or ITP. If you specify types of input desired, you increase the likelihood of participation. For example, there are a number of ways parents can be involved in conducting functional behavior assessments (Peck Peterson, Derby, Berg, & Horner, 2002). Derby and colleagues (1997) helped parents of children with problem behavior conduct functional analyses in the home, which included completing daily behavior logs. "In all cases, parents were able to provide the experimenters with useful information and to conduct analyses that provided information as to the function of the child's problem behavior" (Derby et al., p. 7).

> This type of confrontation really means getting to the heart of the matter and listening to the parent.

In addition, ask parents to raise one or two specific questions at your next team meeting, to give their opinion on their child's progress, or to read about the program being offered so you can discuss it.

Similarly, ask parents to engage in specific tasks rather than admonishing them to be more involved. Providing a specific activity with clear directions for parent and student increases the likelihood that it will be carried out. For example, rather than telling parents to read with their child, give them a book or article to read with their child. Provide a list of discussion questions to guide parents. By supporting home activities in these ways, you increase the likelihood that the parent will have a positive experience and will want to repeat it. At the secondary school level, teachers can raise parents' confidence in their abilities to make an impact by providing information on how to select courses and plan for careers. Alternatively, ask them to help their adolescent become an expert on their IEP to help prepare for transition planning (parents will become experts in the process).

It has been stated that "around 95 percent of school communication is one-way, with school officials telling parents what they or their children should be doing" (Jones, 2001, p. 21). Most parents, regardless of their ethnic or socioeconomic backgrounds, have opinions on what happens to their children in school. Encourage them to share their genuine concerns and address them as much as you can.

Principle 4: Help Parents Participate

Some parents are not able to participate as you request because of realistic concerns, such as being unable to leave their job for a conference or not having help babysitting their children. Asking parents, "Is there anything we can do to make it easier for you to attend meetings (complete the paperwork, etc.)," will give you a window into legitimate obstacles to participation. As much as possible, try to remove these obstacles to make parents' participation easier. For example, Kaufman (2001) suggests maintaining an up-to-date list of community resources (along with addresses and phone numbers) to give to parents. This may include local organizations that provide services to recent immigrants, crisis aid groups, and English as a Second Language classes. In special cases, you might consider offering to alleviate some of their concerns yourself. For example, you and another teacher might take turns sharing childcare responsibilities so you can meet with a parent (meanwhile the other children might enjoy helping the other teacher with classroom tasks). It is also important to invite the parent to bring a family member or friend to help translate if desired. Although the school should provide translators, parents may feel more comfortable with someone they know and trust. Use translated materials and avoid jargon.

In addition, give parents a brief overview of the purpose of your meeting so they know what to expect and understand why they need to attend. In a study of general education teachers, Menlove found that general education teachers often did not attend IEP meetings because "all too often, no one talks to them before IEP meetings to preview what will happen in the meeting, what their role will be, and what information to bring. The teachers often don't know how to prepare for the meeting" (Menlove et al., 2001, p. 31).

Imagine how parents, outsiders to the education system, must feel. Menlove et al. (2001) give the following suggestions regarding IEP meetings:

1. Use an IEP meeting agenda to organize IEP meetings.

2. Distribute the agenda with prior notice to IEP team members to preview what will happen at the meeting and reduce time discussing the agenda during the meeting.

3. Improve communication . . . by letting teachers know ahead of time what will be discussed during the meeting and helpful information they can bring to the meeting. (p. 31)

Although the researchers intended these suggestions to help general educators, they are also applicable to trying to reach nonparticipatory parents.

Some districts, such as the Sacramento Unified School District, compensate teachers (an average of $25 an hour) for making home visits to hard-to-reach families (Jones, 2001). This may be an option for working with select families.

SUGGESTIONS FOR INCREASING PARENT PARTICIPATION IN TRANSITION PLANNING

Parent participation has been identified as one of the primary determinants of success in transition programs (McNair & Rusch, 1991). Unfortunately, as in other areas of special education, teachers often view parents as being uninvolved in transition planning. Often this is because of parents' failure to attend meetings or engage in other formal communication about transition planning. This is disheartening to professionals who feel that, at best, parents are too busy to participate and, at worst, parents do not care. Yet as has been previously discussed, nonparticipation does not necessarily mean noninvolvement.

Research has found that parents are invested in their children's futures and engaged in transition planning at home. Specifically, Morningstar, Turnbull, and Turnbull (1995) conducted focus groups with adolescents who had learning disabilities, emotional or behavioral disorders, or mild mental retardation. They found that families were "the primary source of future planning," particularly with regard to adolescents' career aspirations and plans for independent living (p. 254). Some parents overtly influenced their children, such as with one teenager who stated,

> My mom wants us not to be like her, so she'll go do what she has to so we can get a good education and go to college and stuff like that. And she said she'll kick our butt if we drop out of school. (p. 255)

The majority, however, reported that they had not had any formal discussions with family members about their careers. Instead, they looked to family members (both immediate and extended family) as role models. Similarly, "the issue of family supports [e.g., living with an uncle] often influenced decisions about where a student might go for postsecondary education and training" (p. 252).

Parents of culturally and linguistically diverse groups particularly experience school professionals' negative evaluation of their involvement in transition planning. However, one study found that although African American parents did not attend meetings, they "placed significantly more importance on talking to their children about life after high school and teaching their children to use transportation than did European-American parents" (Geenen et al., 2001, p. 265). In addition, African American, Hispanic, and Native American parents ranked the importance of teaching their children about family values much higher than both European American parents and school professionals (Geenen et al.). Furthermore, Geenen et al. found that "the level of participation reported by culturally and linguistically diverse parents surpassed that of European-American parents" (p. 277). The researchers postulate that for many culturally and linguistically diverse families, "the 'launching' of a young person into adulthood stems from family and community rather than experiences provided by educational or other formal institutions" (p. 279). Consequently, although they see school-based planning as important, it is only one area in which they are preparing their child.

Clearly defining parent responsibilities and formalizing the agreement to participate can contribute to increased parent involvement (Stowitschek et al., 2001). This can be done on an individual or schoolwide basis, where parents are given information about the transition planning process, invited to contribute specific information and attend specific meetings, and asked to sign an agreement about these responsibilities. For example, parents can be asked to do the following:

(a) Provide information on the students' strengths, aspirations, and experiences
(b) Determine priorities among transition goals
(c) Inform the ITP team of family values that impact transition planning

It is also important to include family careers as an aspect of the school vocational curriculum, since students may find these to be more relevant than school-based vocational training (Morningstar et al., 1995). Similarly, identifying family members as sources of support (e.g., living with or sharing transportation with a relative) during transition planning is another realistic and meaningful way to increase involvement, since "very few students mentioned accessing professional support from the adult service system to assist them in their daily living needs" (Morningstar et al., p. 258). In addition, giving parents "user-friendly information on school and community services is one major strategy in supporting family involvement" (Johnson, Stodden, Emanuel, Luecking, & Mack, 2002, p. 529).

The adolescents in Morningstar et al.'s (1995) study felt families should be involved by

(a) Making sure that they stay in high school
(b) Planning for and helping pay for college
(c) Helping them move out on their own
(d) Helping them find a job

as well as spending time talking to them and helping them with their homework.

Research has also found that the amount of collaboration between home and school depends on the level of severity of the student's needs. Specifically, often there is little overt emphasis on transition and minimal interagency involvement for students with mild disabilities (Stowitschek et al., 2001). Thus, professionals may need to adjust their expectations for parent participation depending upon the students' disabilities and needs.

OTHER STRATEGIES FOR DEALING WITH NONPARTICIPATION

While a good relationship is the best antidote to absentee parents, a few other strategies can help include the parent who fails to show up on multiple occasions. Call parents the day before (and if necessary, the day of) the appointment to remind them of the time and location of the meeting. Some people truly forget about their appointments because of other concerns, disorganization, and the like. For example, one single-parent father repeatedly forgot to attend scheduled meetings to discuss his daughter's need for social skills training. He also frequently lost paperwork and failed to bring requested documents. In this case, his drug-abusing background was more responsible for his poor memory than a lack of desire to help his beloved daughter.

If the parent fails to arrive within the first 10 or 15 minutes of the scheduled appointment, immediately call and ask why the parent is not present. "It is important for the staff to be friendly and not accusatory during those phone calls" (Jacob, 2002, p. 21). Rather, the tone should be one of understanding, such as "I'm calling to see if you are running late or if something has come up," so that parents do not feel condemned for failing to attend. Encourage the parent to come, even if they will be quite late, or reschedule for the next day. Have the parent suggest an appropriate time (or give them a few choices) and accommodate their request as much as possible.

Finally, consider whether the situation really requires face-to-face contact. Would it be possible to have a telephone conference and to mail paperwork? Some parents may be grateful for this option. Remember to retain copies of any paperwork you send.

OTHER STRATEGIES FOR DEALING WITH RESISTANCE

At times parents may be quite resistant to your suggestions and interventions, such as specific class placements or interventions. Rather than state their disagreement outright, they may use other means of expressing their resistance, such as by being uncooperative or failing to follow through. Vera Kishinevsky, a veteran teacher and school psychologist in New York, recalls working with one challenging family where multiple letters, phone calls, and a visit occurred before the parent finally agreed to meet with the school. Further parental resistance thwarted the school's efforts to help the child. She relates the following story:

> Myesha was initially placed in special education due to behavioral issues. In second grade, she acted out in class while her father was going through a nasty divorce process. . . . At the time of our contact [at her triennial evaluation at age 15], Myesha's school progress was very good and her behavior significantly improved. [We] decided to help Myesha transfer to a local small leadership academy where she would get a chance to apply her above average intelligence and exceptional abilities and get support she needed for transition to general education.
>
> During the Educational Planning Conference, Myesha's stepmother looked surprised when she heard praise and admiration for Myesha's resilience and maturation. She took note of the team's recommendations and promised to follow up. . . . The Educational Planning Conference took place in March. After seven (!) failed appointments for which she had various excuses, the stepmother refused to talk to the School Based Support Team at all. Myesha stayed in the same large inner-city high school where she felt betrayed and abandoned. In October, the stepmother came to our office and triumphantly announced, "I received this letter from the attendance office because Myesha cuts classes. She missed 15 days since the beginning of the semester." She obviously enjoyed rubbing our faces in our "mistake" and claimed that Myesha had never been "up to any good" and it would have been a "waste of my time to worry about her getting into that fancy school."

This stepmother's resistance probably stemmed from personal issues rather than a difference of opinion or educational judgment. Reasoning with such parents is unlikely to change their uncooperativeness. Instead, attempt to understand the parent's resistance and speak to the underlying concerns. For example, perhaps this stepmother needed to share the spotlight and some praise for her success in raising Myesha would have helped her cooperate. Research suggests that being supportive and nonconfrontational is more effective than more directive approaches at circumventing resistance, such as challenging the parent (Beutler, Moliero, & Talebi, 2002). In hindsight, Dr. Kishinevsky also wonders whether more attempts to involve the father would have changed the outcome for Myesha. Similarly, involving other staff, including paraprofessionals, who may have a closer relationship with the resistant parent than you do, may be helpful.

Be aware that culture and socioeconomic status can also play a part in parents' resistance.

> Parents who do not believe that they can challenge school authorities are likely to withdraw from participation. Out of a traditional respect for authority, however, they may continue to defer to professionals, yet fail to cooperate with professional recommendations or even respond to invitations to participate. (Harry, 1992a, p. 475)

One area in which cultural values and SES have been found to play a role in parents' resistance is the use of assistive technology services or devices. For example, Parette and McMahan (2002) present a case study of a close-knit Hispanic family in which four generations of the family reside within a few blocks of one another. When an IEP team member suggested that the daughter, who has mental retardation, could benefit from physical and occupational therapy to increase her independence, "the parents grew quiet on hearing this recommendation, noting the feeling that Maria will most likely remain at home as she grows older and be taken care of by her family" (p. 57).

Similarly, the "introduction of many assistive technology devices into family settings may result in increased stress for family members, frustration, and other potentially negative effects" (Parette & McMahan, 2002, p. 60). For example, families may not be able to commit the time or financial resources to be trained to use assistive technology or may not have the means to transport an assistive technology device (e.g., mobility aids). Parette and McMahan describe the difficulties a Native American family faced in utilizing their daughter's manual wheelchair:

> [White Dove's] family—two parents, four children, and two grandparents—typically compact themselves into the family automobile to visit relatives on the nearby reservation. Given the amount of luggage that must be transported, the family noted that it would not be practical for them to carry a wheelchair in the trunk of the car during these routine visits and that the father would prefer to transport White Dove in his arms. (p. 61)

Educators may need to coax these parents into sharing their thoughts, such as by asking respectful open-ended questions (e.g., "Are there reasons why you may not want to use assistive technology outside your home?") or by enlisting other staff (who may or may not share their background) to talk with them.

WHAT TO AVOID

At some point, repeated requests turn into pressure, and pressure results in a defensive (and possibly hostile) parent. If you sense that a power struggle is developing between you (or the school) and the parent, it is time to back off. The more you push, the less likely it is that you will receive cooperation and the more likely it is that you will reinforce a negative image of school professionals. Give the uncooperative parent some time to change before approaching the issue again. For example, one mother repeatedly refused to heed the school's recommendations for her daughter's learning disabilities. Any suggestions seemed to go in one ear and out the other. After the parent missed a few meetings, the teacher once again made an appointment for Tuesday night, the usual day for parent conferences in her school. The next day, the teacher happened to see the parent in the grocery store and commented on her repeated absences. The mother angrily retorted, "What is it with you people? I told you, I'm not coming on Tuesdays. That's when my favorite TV show is on and I'm not going to miss it to meet with you!"

Was this mother a callous, uncaring parent? Not quite. She had an older son, also a student with special needs requiring a great deal of attention. At the same time, she was pregnant with her third child. Exhausted, she couldn't handle much more and was turned off by so many people demanding more from her and insisting that she was not doing enough. The television show was the one hour a week she had carved out to take care of herself. Showing support and genuine concern over time (such as by asking, "You must be so exhausted; do you have anyone to help you with the kids?") eventually softened her enough so that she could begin to talk realistically about what she could and could not do for her daughter. Continually dealing with a child's problems at school can be tiring and frustrating for parents. Patience and more appropriate timing can be your allies.

Avoid blaming the parent or otherwise expressing negative judgment. At the height of her frustration, one teacher made the mistake of telling a parent who repeatedly refused to have her son placed in a special class, "What you're doing is really educational neglect." As you might expect, the parent was offended and became even more opposed to the school's recommendations. Even if the parent bears some responsibility for a negative outcome, blaming him or her will not elicit cooperation.

Similarly, do not make dire predictions about the future to coerce the parent. Saying things like, "If Ryan isn't put into this special class, he will never be able to function independently" is not only unkind, it may also be untrue. It is hard to predict the future, and stories abound of parents being told their disabled children would never walk, talk, and so forth, who later became successful adults.

GOING BEYOND NONPARTICIPATION AND RESISTANCE

Let's face it, there are some parents who, despite your valiant efforts, will not come to their appointments and will not become more openly involved in their children's education. It is not your responsibility to heal past educational hurts or rehabilitate the parent. If you are unsuccessful in getting a nonparticipatory parent to cooperate with you, change your goal. Since the child will be in school for many years to come, you can focus on motivating the parent to participate in the future. Be gracious rather than condemning. You might send a note saying, "I wish I had had the opportunity to meet with you. I know you have a lot to offer. Perhaps when time and circumstances allow. . . ." As one teacher put it, you are a link in a very long chain. If parent involvement and teamwork do not happen with you, that does not mean it will not happen in the future. Showing kindness with a nonparticipatory parent now may just help another teacher later on.

REFLECTING ON YOUR TEACHING

You can probably identify at least one parent who you feel is not as involved as he or she should be. Use the following questions and activities to reflect on your teaching and to guide you in forming a plan to reach your nonparticipatory parents.

1. How much do you want parents to be involved? Do you enjoy autonomy and being the one who calls the shots?

2. How does your school help or hinder parent involvement?

3. Identify specific steps you can take to increase the participation of culturally and linguistically diverse parents.

4. Are there any groups or types of parents you find it difficult to communicate and be involved with? How can obstacles to involvement be addressed?

5. In what ways have you tried to get to know the parents of your students (e.g., on a personal basis, only when needed)?

SUMMARY

Teachers differ widely on how they view a lack of parent participation. Some see it as problematic, others are relieved, and still others have given little thought to involving parents. Similarly, parents have many and varied reasons for not participating more fully in their children's education. These include parents who are put off by formal education, parents who do not fully understand the benefits of participating, and parents who are unable to be more involved for valid reasons. Parents from culturally and linguistically diverse groups may also limit their participation due to mistrust or different views of the roles of educators. Parents of adolescents may be unaware of how to be involved in developmentally appropriate ways. Four strategies for gaining cooperation from nonparticipatory parents are (1) getting to know the parents, (2) finding creative ways to develop relationships with parents, (3) listening to parents' underlying concerns, and (4) addressing parents' realistic problems. In addition, there are ways to be supportive with parents who are resistant or frequently do not appear for appointments. A long-term perspective must be taken when helping parents who resist all efforts to become more involved. With these parents, you may focus instead on setting a positive tone for future participation.

DEALING WITH MISTRUST

*"The mother declined the recommendation ...
and kept insisting that the School Based Support
Team was discriminating against her child and was
making an unfair and racist recommendation."*

Vera Kishinevsky, Ph.D.
School Psychologist
15 years of teaching experience
Bronx, NY

I f parents challenge your instructional choices or classroom practices, you may be able to change their views by citing district guidelines, recounting a few anecdotes, or even giving statistics. But what if their criticisms are personal rather than professional? How can you address parents' accusations that you dislike their child? Or that you treat their child differently because he is poor? Or that you are narrow-minded and racist? When parents question your intentions and motives, you may be offended on both a professional and a personal level. Getting these types of parents to trust you may be more complicated and problematic than dealing with their educational concerns.

> Trust is the foundation for any collaborative relationship.

Trust is the foundation for any collaborative relationship. Mistrust between parents and teachers has profound consequences. Whether trust has been eroded because of a specific offense or because the parent is mistrusting in general, steps need to be taken to restore faith in each other.

RECOGNIZING THE VALUE OF TRUST

When trust is intact, people tend to tolerate or overlook periodic problems. If parents believe that you and others are genuinely acting in the best interests of their children, they are able to give school personnel the benefit of the doubt. Rather than being suspicious, they reserve judgment and do not make too much of any single negative event. For example, one educator mistakenly believed (and told other teachers) that a student had been put on medication for ADHD. The parents clarified he had not and dismissed the incident as a simple misunderstanding.

In contrast, without a foundation of trust, parents feel they must question everything, from seemingly innocuous suggestions to special education placements. If the parents in the previous example had not trusted the teacher, they might have become upset and charged that school personnel were spreading vicious rumors about their child. Some parent publications feed on this adversarial tone. Titles such as *You, Your Child and Special Education: A Guide to Making the System Work* (Cutler, 1993), and *From Emotions to Advocacy: The Special Education Survival Guide* (Wright & Wright, 2001) suggest that parents should be wary and cannot trust schools. Some give suggestions that put parents in a guarded mindset and defensive posture. For instance, Cutler's book advises parents to bring witnesses to school meetings so the school cannot shortchange them.

Once trust is broken, it may be very difficult for parents to trust again. In Lake and Billingsley's (2000) interviews of parents of students with special needs, parents in broken trust relationships reported that they lacked the confidence to fully accept school personnel's demonstration of good-faith efforts. After a point, they no longer maintained hope that the parent-school relationship had value in and of itself or provided benefit to the child. Parents reported turning points in their ability to trust. . . . It was at this point that parents requested out-of-district placements, changes of schools, mediation or due process hearings. (p. 248)

Unfortunately, even if you were not responsible for the breakdown of trust, parents may group you with other school professionals whom they distrust.

UNDERSTANDING MISTRUST

Parents have some legitimate reasons for not trusting the education system overall and special education in particular. One longstanding issue at the core of some parents' mistrust is that of minority overrepresentation in special education. For the past three decades, African Americans, particularly males, have been disproportionately represented in classes for serious behavioral or emotional disorders and mental retardation (Artiles & Trent, 1994; Gollnick & Chinn, 1994; Harry & Anderson, 1994). Although African Americans constitute 16% of the public school population, they make up 28% of all students in special education (National Clearinghouse for Professions in Special Education, 1991), including 34% of the children in programs for mental retardation (Council for Exceptional Children, 1994). While the reality of minority overrepresentation has been increasingly acknowledged, these statistics have stayed relatively stable since the 1970s (Patton, 1998).

Some might wonder whether these disparate numbers are inherently problematic. As one researcher commented,

That is not a question that I have ever heard an African American special educator, sociologist, psychologist, anthropologist, barber, teacher, minister, social worker, custodian, businessperson, homemaker, or anyone else ask. Nor have I heard Latinos or Native Americans ask that question. We know the answer and it is *yes*. (Patton, 1998, p. 30, italics in original)

Not all parents of culturally diverse backgrounds may hold this view, but many do. This leads some parents to charge that the school system at large is guilty of racial discrimination and violations of civil rights, particularly for African American youth.

Some parents may see the education system as "designed to serve the interests of the dominant social, political, and economic classes and to place African Americans in a disvalued position" (Patton, 1998, p. 27). As representatives of the greater system, teachers may bear the brunt of parents' mistrust. Many note that the subjectivity of teacher judgments in the referral process contributes to disproportionate referral and special education placement of African American students (see Patton). Parents may accuse you of being racist, simply because you represent the dominant culture.

Racism is both real and perceived. Arthur Ashe, the late tennis player and activist, was quoted as saying that "the toughest obstacle he faced was not his two open heart surgeries, or even AIDS, but rather, as he put it, 'being born black in America'" (Dell, 2003, p. 7). Anyone who has been the victim of blatant racism (e.g., being called epithets by strangers) and discrimination (e.g., being denied a job or promotion) can become sensitive to more subtle forms of racism, as well as perceive racism where none exists. When African American, Hispanic, and other parents are given less-than-satisfactory reasons for why their children are being placed in special classes or denied services, it is understandable that some would suspect they are the targets of racism. Parents' experiences as schoolchildren are also likely to impact how they address racism with their children. For example, some Hispanics' "lingering distrust of educators stems from the fact that [they] . . . were *hit* for speaking in Spanish" (Jones, 2001, p. 21, italics in original). Teaching about racial identity and racism is a core issue in African American parenting (Mosley-Howard & Evans, 2000), which may result in students harboring the same mistrust as their parents.

In truth, multiple factors account for the overrepresentation of African Americans in special education, only some of which involve teachers. Some suggest that teacher preparation programs, and thus teachers, adhere to a Eurocentric framework (Talbert-Johnson, 1998) and share the same values and expectations of the dominant Anglo-Saxon Protestant macro culture (Spindler & Spindler, 1994). As a result, all students, despite their cultures, languages, and values, are expected to conform to the norm. Students who do not match this Eurocentric picture are consequently identified as deviant. For example, students' communication styles (e.g., volume, tone) may be culturally consistent, but may be deemed inappropriate in the classroom. Similarly, "misclassification of culturally diverse students in special education . . . may result when the behavioral expectations differ between culturally diverse students' homes and school environments" (Aaroe & Nelson, 2000, pp. 314–315). This is exacerbated by the fact that while the number of students of diverse cultures is steadily increasing, the teaching force remains largely Caucasian (see Aaroe & Nelson).

One study comparing African American children and European American children found that adaptive skills, such as communication, socialization, and daily living skills, significantly predicted academic achievement (e.g., grades and standardized test scores) for European American children (Brady, Tucker, Harris, & Tribble, 1992). However, only *maladaptive* behavior (e.g., acting out) predicted academic achievement for

African American children. This suggests a real discrepancy in the way African American children are viewed by some educators, lending credibility to parents' charges of racism. Similarly, parents of other cultures may be suspicious of why their children are referred for special education. One study of Mexican Americans found the following:

> For the most part, they didn't perceive their children as having learning disabilities; rather, they cited the following reasons for placement . . . "intimidated by the other children who called her names because she was fat and dark-skinned," "he was not behaving well at home and at school," and, most commonly, "she never liked to go to school." (Hayes, 1992, p. 261)

ACKNOWLEDGING OTHER REASONS FOR PARENTAL MISTRUST

The bureaucracy and the hierarchy of the public education system also contribute to parental mistrust. Parents may become wary when passed on from professional to professional, many of whom claim they have no authority or power to grant what the parent is requesting. As a result, parents may be skeptical of specific professionals who seem to present more obstacles than assistance. One parent who was unsuccessful in team meetings and in mediation stated,

> My thought process on it was that the head of the special education department is the pit bull to keep parents away from the superintendent. Once you get past the pit bull, then something can happen. (Lake & Billingsley, 2000, p. 248)

Some parents suspect their children are denied services for financial reasons. In Lake and Billingsley's (2000) interviews of parents, parents became suspicious when "no one could truthfully state that lack of services was due to lack of funds, [and] other reasons were offered to parents" (p. 246). Parents may believe that school personnel are withholding optimum treatment or recommending subpar services in order to save the district money or to siphon money to other students.

Parents also may become mistrustful when they feel the teacher is narrow-mindedly focusing on an issue or suggesting interventions. One mother was distressed that her son's kindergarten teacher repeatedly told her to have him evaluated by his pediatrician for ADHD. Although the teacher knew that she could not make a specific recommendation for medication, she was convinced (based on past experience) that the child needed to be on medication to calm his boisterousness. The mother was outraged that the teacher had not offered to meet with her to identify problems and brainstorm solutions and instead had made a snap judgment about her son. Another parent, a nurse, was devastated when her son's teacher told her he was autistic after having known him for just a few days. She felt the teacher had not taken the time to get to know her son or the reasons behind his reticence and was making a hasty judgment about her son's language delay, one that could have profound effects on her son's education. In both of these cases, the parents concluded that the teacher was untrustworthy and would not treat their children properly.

Parents also become wary if they feel they as parents are being judged unfairly or blamed for their children's problems. One low-income African American mother commented,

> She is judging *me*. I met this lady once, *one time,* and she judged me . . . she kept saying [my son's] environment is making him act like that. [But] I am his environment. So what is she trying to say? That I am not a good mother or something? (Kalyanpur & Rao, 1991, p. 527, italics in original)

As educators, it is easy to think that a child's learning or behavior problems may stem from his or her chaotic home life. However, parents who feel they, their culture, or their lifestyles are being blamed understandably become suspicious of their accusers, wondering whether educators are being objective in their assessment of the child and doing all *they* can to help the student.

Parents who themselves have had negative experiences with school may carry this skepticism and mistrust into their children's schooling. For example, in one study, African American parents were reluctant to initiate a conference with their child's teacher to discuss their concerns, despite the seriousness of their concerns (Garlington, 1991). Their reaction stemmed from their childhood experiences of poor communication with teachers. Other parents who had learning or behavioral problems as children may also be suspicious of interventions for their children. For example, one mother reflected on the school's handling of her son's learning and attentional problems:

> My son is a lot like I was at his age. I was left back in the third grade and it made me feel even more stupid. I will never forget the beginning of the next school year when my friends moved up to fourth grade but I stayed in third. . . . I wish I could say that repeating the grade helped me to learn better. . . . It wasn't until I began to get the kind of help I needed when I was in high school that I was able to keep up. (R. Brooks, personal communication, November 4, 2002)

It is plausible that this mother would reject any recommendations for her son that were similar to interventions used with her.

Still others might treat their children's teachers with suspicion due to their general discomfort with or dislike of school. This may have been the case with one mother who accused Adele Unterberg, an elementary art teacher, unjustly. She recounts:

> One morning in the middle of a lesson, my classroom phone rang. I ran to answer only to hear, "My son has a knot on his head, and it happened in your room." I stood there dumbfounded. I teach numerous classes and have hundreds of students.
>
> "Who are you? Who is this?" I asked, shocked at the tone of voice.
>
> "This is Steve's mother. He has a big knot, and you did nothing."
>
> This is a parent who has never met me, never came to see her child's work, and never once came to visit during the teacher-parent events. Her son was now in the upper grades and I've been teaching him for over five years. Yet for this situation, she had time to carry on and to blame. It turned out that his "knot" did not happen in my room, nor was he innocent of the incident that caused his injury.

AGREEING ON AN INDIVIDUAL TRANSITION PLAN

Several aspects of transition planning in particular may arouse mistrust in some parents. First, the IDEA Amendments of 1997 clearly state that families must be encouraged to be involved in transition planning for students with special needs. As previously noted, parent participation in ITP meetings is often minimal or passive (Collet-Klingenberg, 1998). This leads to well-intentioned educators taking the lead (with or without the student's input) in setting ITP goals and objectives, which includes course selection and identification of necessary skills. Unfortunately, parents may be resentful of school staff imposing a future on their children, especially if parents feel the school has low expectations for their child. For example, one mother was upset that her son, who has learning disabilities, was discouraged from becoming a surgeon. School staff felt that because of the severity of his organizational and learning problems, he would not be able to complete medical school. Instead, they encouraged him to become a dental assistant or nurses' aide.

This resentment may be felt particularly strongly by parents of culturally and linguistically diverse backgrounds. Overall mistrust of the system and divergent values may lead some parents to question whether their child is being typecast into an "appropriate" occupation based on racial or ethnic stereotypes. Some parents may be suspicious that school staff are deliberately denying their child the opportunity to obtain a high school diploma based on prejudice. In reality, staff may be more concerned with the fact that students are no longer entitled to special education services once a standard high school diploma is granted (Johnson, Stodden, Emanuel, Luecking, & Mack, 2002).

Similarly, the prevailing emphasis on student participation and self-determination may be at odds with some cultural group norms. Self-determination refers to a person's freedom to make decisions (e.g., about work or education) independently (Schloss, Alper, & Jayne, 1994). Embedded within self-determination are cultural values of independence, autonomy, and equity (Harry, Rueda, & Kalyanpur, 1999), values that are ingrained in the dominant American culture. Collectivistic cultures (e.g., Asian), however, tend to value interdependence more than autonomy, and expectations for family members vary accordingly. Thus, a family that adheres to traditional Chinese values may not expect their daughter to leave home at age 18. She may be expected to live with her parents until she marries or may be expected to live with them indefinitely if her disabilities are significant. Indeed, "evidence that . . . culturally and linguistically diverse parents support self-determination is sparse" (Trainor, 2002, p. 723). Parents may also be uncomfortable with the school allowing their child to play a leadership role in an ITP meeting if their cultural norms dictate deferring to elders and experts in hierarchical relationships.

A third issue in transition planning that may contribute to parental mistrust is the time frame for transition planning. For transition planning to be successful, discussions must begin early. For example, although the goal may be to live independently, numerous short-term objectives and annual goals must be reached before the eventual goal of one's own apartment can be fulfilled. A drawback of beginning early, however, is that some parents may be wary of limiting their child's opportunities. For example, a parent of an adolescent with mental retardation may be dismayed to see that the long-range employment goal is to work in a supermarket upon graduation.

Educators can avoid these potential areas of mistrust by actively engaging parents in the transition planning process and sensitively exploring parents' values. Although IDEA 1997 only requires ITPs beginning at the age of 14, interventions can begin even at the elementary level. For example, parents can be informed about the ITP process while their children are in late elementary or middle school in order to prompt dialogue (not to actually make plans). Family interviews conducted on a regular basis can help parents explore options in a more nonthreatening manner (Hutchins & Renzaglia, 1998). Steere and Cavaiuolo (2002) also advise that ITP "team members do not limit ideas unnecessarily without first attempting to determine possible avenues for attaining the outcome," such as actual community experience (p. 57). Since no one can predict the future, it is best to let students' experiences (e.g., while job shadowing) indicate whether goals are inappropriate. Parents and students can also be encouraged to reflect on their experiences and aspirations together, through assignments or informal discussions. For example, students may be directed to interview a family member on their transition to adulthood through questions such as "When you were my age, how did you envision your life? How did you try to achieve your goals?"

In addition, remember that ITPs should include goals for leisure pursuits as well as occupational and educational realms. It may be easier to begin the ITP process by discussing recreation and leisure pursuits, which are less controversial than educational or occupational goals. Leisure pursuits enhance the quality of life, social skills, and relationships of students with special needs and require similar foresight and planning as occupational and educational goals (Modell & Valdez, 2002). For example, if the student's desire is to participate in a wheelchair basketball league, short-term goals such as independently accessing transportation need to be identified. Interagency coordination or other community links may also need to be put in place. Going through the process of discussing recreation and leisure pursuits helps parents and school professionals become comfortable with one another and with the ins and outs of putting together an ITP.

PREVENTING MISTRUST

In your relationships with parents, remember that trust is the one indispensable quality you must maintain. Other areas, including communication, problem solving, and decision making, all hinge upon trust. Above all, safeguard trust with your parents. Be sure to "respond to conflicts early, before trust is broken" (Lake & Billingsley, 2000, p. 250). It is much easier to restore a fragile sense of trust with parents than to try to win back parents' faith after they have initiated legal proceedings. Make each parent feel like he or she is respected and valued.

How can you accomplish this with parents whose backgrounds are so different from your own? We all have a natural bias against people who are different from ourselves. Sociologists and psychologists term this the *in-group/out-group bias*. Judgments about out-group members (the not-like-me group) tend to be extreme and polarized (e.g., "Those people are lazy and undependable"), whereas we are more forgiving toward people we view as similar to ourselves (Forsyth, 1990). Even if you and the parents share the same ethnic background, your college degree alone places you in a small category of people, leaving the majority of the population in the out-group. Only a quarter of the general population in 2000 had completed college; this decreases to 16.5% of African Americans and 10% of Hispanics (Wright, 2001). Though you may not be able to relate on a personal level with someone from a different cultural or socioeconomic background, being respectful, opening up to them, and trying to understand their perspectives helps forge relationships. Attempts to learn about an immigrant's culture or language, for example, are likely to establish goodwill with parents and to shore up trust.

Although you do not have to bear your soul, be honest as much as is appropriate. If the parents (and you) suspect that fiscal concerns are at the root of the district's reluctance to provide services, do not pretend this is not a possibility. When the parent charges, "This school cares more about money than my child," you can acknowledge their beliefs without being dismissive (or contributing to a lawsuit). You can say, "I honestly don't know if financial concerns are a part of this; it's possible. But we do want to provide what your daughter needs."

At the same time, if parents ask you a question that you should know the answer to but do not, be truthful. Rather than skirt the issue or talk your way out of the situation, you might say, "I'm glad you asked. I really should know the answer, but I don't. Let me find out and I will call you tomorrow." Being upfront is essential to maintaining trust, since parents often believe that the "inability to answer their questions about services was an indicator that something was amiss with how services were actually being given to a child" (Lake & Billingsley, 2000, p. 245).

Communicate often and as clearly as possible, avoiding the use of jargon, which may unintentionally create distrust. Harry, Allen, and McLaughlin (1995) cite a situation in which a mother was informed her daughter needed to be moved to a Level 5 placement to accommodate her health needs.

> The mother, focusing on the positive aspects of small class size, agreed to the decision, but did not really understand the implications of a more restrictive placement. She expressed shock when she discovered that the center was 10 miles and two bus changes away, in a segregated school for children with physical and cognitive difficulties that she perceived to be more severe than her daughter's. (p. 372)

Unexplained jargon and inadequate information can lead to misunderstandings that may be interpreted by parents as deliberate attempts to deceive them.

The importance of good communication cannot be overstated. Research has found that inadequate provision of information and over-reliance on formalized written communication contributed to parents' mistrust and withdrawal (Harry 1992a). Recalling "the worst experience of my teaching career," Mary Ellen Allen, an educator with 8 years of teaching experience, states that better communication with the parent, her colleagues, and administrators may have been helpful in dealing with an unusually volatile mother.

Her child was extremely shy and I tried everything I could think of to warm her into participating in class. She wouldn't even read aloud to me beyond a whisper. One day after school when the student and her mom were in my classroom, the little girl was running around with her little brother. I made the comment to her mother that that was the loudest I had ever heard the little girl speak. . . .

The mother was infuriated that I was the teacher and had never heard her daughter's normal speaking voice. It was all on me and not her daughter. She went straight to the superintendent, wrote an article in the newspaper . . . she came totally unglued. Parents of my other students protected me from her and never left me alone. If that mom walked into the classroom, so did they. In the end a. meeting was called with administrators, psychologists and a superintendent representative. The mom screamed at me the whole time. . . . When it was over they concluded that the mom was psycho.

Allen states that teachers faced with similar situations should "be confident about the ways and whats you teach and be ready to *explain* it (not defend it). The teacher is the professional and your administrator, if informed, is there to support you."

MAIN PRINCIPLES FOR DEALING WITH MISTRUST

At some point, you may be faced with having to repair a broken relationship with parents who have become distrustful of the school in general or of you in particular. The following three guiding principles are the basics of reestablishing trust once it has been broken.

Principle 1: Acknowledge Mistrust Openly

Expert negotiators Roger Fisher and William Ury of the Harvard Negotiation Project suggest making emotions explicit and acknowledging them as legitimate.

Making your feelings or theirs an explicit focus of discussion will not only underscore the seriousness of the problem, it will also make the negotiations less reactive and more proactive. Freed from the burden of unexpressed emotions, people will become more likely to work on the problem. (Fisher et al., 1991, p. 30)

Table 6.1	Main Principles for Dealing With Mistrust
Principle 1: Acknowledge Mistrust Openly	
Principle 2: Make Amends	
Principle 3: Find Common Ground	

This means saying to a parent, "After all that's happened, I wonder if it is hard for you to trust me or anyone else at this school." This gives parents the opportunity to discuss their mistrust, and chances are, they do not want to be suspicious and would welcome the opportunity to restore trust. Parents may want to vent about the many reasons why the school has lost their trust, and providing a listening ear may suffice. If parents acknowledge their mistrust and state that they will continue to distrust you, be as gracious as you can. You may need to say, "I'm sorry to hear that. I hope that over time, as we work together, you will feel able to trust me."

You can also encourage distrustful parents to bring a friend or other family member to meetings you have. This acknowledges the parents' need for support and conveys you have nothing to hide. At the same time, a third party may help restore the parents' objectivity, since the friend may be more rational than the parent. The possibility exists that this friend may make the situation worse; you have to judge whether it is worth the risk.

Principle 2: Make Amends

Fisher et al. (1991) also suggest using symbolic gestures to restore strained relationships. These may include a statement of regret, shaking hands, and making an apology. According to these experts, "An apology may be one of the least costly and most rewarding investments you can make" (p. 32). Apologizing does not require that you admit an intention to harm or even acknowledge personal responsibility, though you may need to if indeed you are to blame for the loss of trust.

However, consistency is essential. Your actions must match your words, otherwise you will not be perceived as credible. This means making extra efforts to *be* trustworthy. If you are attempting to restore trust, make that relationship a priority. Grading papers and making photocopies can wait; a doubting parent cannot (and should not). If you say you will talk to someone for the parent, make sure you do. Follow up with the parent immediately to inform him or her of your actions.

Principle 3: Find Common Ground

Initially, finding common ground may seem difficult, and any commonalities may be superficial. However, these small, seemingly insignificant details can help restore trust. For example, noting that you and a parent like the same coffee or listen to the same radio station reminds parents that you are a person (not just the untrustworthy professional they believe you are).

Research has found that the most effective way to get two opposing parties to overlook their differences is to have them focus on superordinate goals, or goals that can only be achieved if the two groups work together (Sherif, Harvey, White, Hood, & Sherif, 1961). "Without cooperation . . . [opposing parties continue] to perceive each other as opponents who must be rejected and defeated" (Forsyth, 1990, p. 415). Cooperation reduces conflict because it reverses us-versus-them thinking. Involve the parent in a joint task for the child's benefit, such as developing a homework plan together or preparing a child for upcoming tests.

If your joint project fails to quell some of the mistrust, you may need to tell a parent that, regardless of their feelings, you still need to work together. In as patient and understanding a manner as possible, say, "Let's remember that we are both here for your daughter and try to work together regardless of our feelings. We don't want her to lose out because you and I are having trouble working together."

OTHER STRATEGIES FOR DEALING WITH MISTRUST

If parents have decided that you are untrustworthy, they may be more receptive to hearing distressing information from someone else. Involve others who may be more successful in working with the parents. Vera Kishinevsky, a school psychologist working in a high school, shares the following story about a 17-year-old:

> Rashid was initially evaluated at the age of 8 and placed in a special education class. His mother was unhappy with his school progress and requested the reevaluation; she insisted that Rashid is in need of Speech and Language services to increase his chances of getting into college. The reevaluation indicated that Rashid's reading and mathematics skills were at the 4.5 and 4.0 grade levels. His IQ was assessed to be within the Borderline range. . . . A Speech and Language evaluation found significant delays. . . .
>
> However, due to his age, the Educational Planning Conference suggested that no additional services be initiated. The mother declined the recommendation that Rashid be transferred to a smaller school with a strong vocational component and kept insisting that the School Based Support Team was discriminating against her child and was making an unfair and racist recommendation.

The conflict between the parent and the School Based Support Team was addressed by sending the case to the Committee on Special Education where the mother seemed more satisfied by the same decision.

In addition, you may want to reduce parents' mistrust by increasing their exposure to you. Encourage the parent to visit the classroom simply to observe. Seeing you, their child, and other students interact in a positive manner may do more to restore trust than any words you can say. However, it behooves you to talk with your colleagues first, since they may know more about the family. In Mary Ellen Allen's case, it became apparent that the mother was "a unique individual" (possibly mentally ill) when "other incidents began to surface." In the few cases in which a parent's mistrust and behavior are extreme, suspiciousness and blame may be part of their psychological makeup. With these individuals, you will probably not be able to change their minds, but should focus instead on being professional and taking care of yourself.

Also, remember to document all pertinent interactions, such as your efforts and interventions used with the child as well as conversations with the parents, to avoid he said–she said arguments with upset parents.

WHAT TO AVOID

When trust has been broken, do not postpone taking action. The longer you wait, the more likely it is that irreparable damage will occur. Address the situation openly and quickly. If you hear rumors that parents are unhappy and have lost their confidence in you, immediately discuss the rumors with the parents to ferret out any nuggets of truth. Do not allow the strained relationship to become (or remain) broken. Parents who are unwilling or unable to trust you are likely to make their feelings known to others. Your lack of response may enable them to plant a seed of mistrust in your relationships with other parents.

For example, one mother felt her son's fifth-grade teacher was unfairly criticizing him and holding him to a higher standard than other students. The teacher discovered this when the student told her, "My mom says you give me a harder time than the other kids." Annoyed but busy, the teacher chose to ignore the remark and never spoke with the mother about the issue. Consequently, the mother continued to bad-mouth the teacher to anyone who would listen. This mother's anger fueled her suspicions, and her son adopted the mother's distrusting posture as well.

GOING BEYOND MISTRUST

While it is tempting to dismiss parents who do not trust you as impossible to work with, consider that your efforts to change their views may yield great rewards. If you can get beyond mistrust into a restored relationship, you are likely to find yourself in a very productive relationship. In part, this is because your communication with these previously mistrusting parents will have been refined through the process of rebuilding your relationship. In addition, you will be focused on working together rather than getting to know each other. Having dealt successfully with an issue as serious as mistrust also means you and the parents have developed effective ways to deal with conflict. Having negotiated these difficult hurdles, these parents may become your staunchest supporters and closest allies.

REFLECTING ON YOUR TEACHING

No one likes to be unjustly accused of wrongdoing or to have his or her morals questioned. Teachers who find themselves in this unpleasant position may be tempted to dismiss the thought of repairing the relationship. Use the following questions and activities to assist you in considering your own relationships with distrustful parents.

1. What experiences have you had with mistrust outside the classroom and how was trust restored?

2. How comfortable do you feel acknowledging and talking about parents' feelings toward you?

3. Are there groups or types of people you feel uncomfortable with or know little about that may cause you to hold stereotypes?

4. What steps can you take to help parents get to know you as a trustworthy individual and professional?

5. Identify specific superordinate goals or a joint project you can work on with a parent who may be distrustful of you.

SUMMARY

System characteristics (such as the bureaucracy of the educational system and the process for transition planning), teacher characteristics (such as making snap judgments and single-mindedly focusing on issues), and parent characteristics (such as negative childhood experiences in education) all contribute to parental mistrust. In addition, historical patterns of overrepresentation of African Americans in special education have resulted in a general sense of mistrust among many ethnic minority parents. Preventing the breakdown of trust by conscientiously building relationships is essential. However, when trust has been eroded, it can be restored by openly acknowledging mistrust, making amends, and focusing on superordinate goals. Restoring trust in a broken relationship should take the utmost priority, as trust serves as the foundation for any working relationship.

WORKING WITH NONTRADITIONAL FAMILIES

"*Every child in my class leaves someone to come to school each day and each child returns to someone. I will fully know and teach that child only when I connect with that someone.*"

Hurt (2000, p. 88)

W hile the general principles presented in the previous chapters are applicable to populations with unique concerns as well, it is helpful to be aware of specific issues faced by grandparents, noncustodial parents, foster parents, and homeless families. These groups have traditionally been challenging for educators, yet they need not be. In addition, as mandated reporters, teachers should be prepared for situations in which they suspect child abuse or neglect may be occurring. With care, your responsibilities for reporting can be met without necessarily sacrificing your relationships with the family.

WORKING WITH GRANDPARENTS

Ten-year-old Calia and her four siblings reside with their grandmother, just blocks away from the drug house where their mother continues to abuse cocaine and alcohol.

Nelson has lived with his grandparents since birth. When his mother abandoned him at a hospital, his grandparents chose to raise him rather than to have him placed in foster care.

Since their parents' divorce, Elena and her brother have lived in their grandparents' home. Their mother, the custodial parent, sees little of them due to her long work hours.

Melina, aged six, lives with her father in her grandmother's home. Melina's parents were teenagers when she was born, and her grandmother took charge of the situation when it appeared Melina would have been put up for adoption.

Damian moved into his grandmother's home when his parents died of AIDS, joining two other cousins who live there because their parents are incarcerated.

In the past, teachers may have encountered one or two grandparents who were active in their students' education. Perhaps these grandparents were an important part of an extended family network. However, now more than ever before teachers are encountering grandparents in the role of the primary caregiver. For all intents and purposes, they are the students' parents. However, because these grandparents face different challenges, they should not be treated as any other parent, but instead be recognized as unique.

Custodial Grandparents

It is estimated that 1 in 20 children under 18 lives in a home headed by a grandparent without the parents present (Glass & Huneycutt, 2002). The prevalence of custodial grandparents is particularly high in New York City, where in 1990, 12.4% of children were being raised by grandparents (U.S. Census Bureau, 1990). Often, these families are poor (Cox, 2000) and have less than a high school education (Rothenberg, 1996).

Although these grandparents choose to raise their grandchildren, most feel as if they did not have a choice, since failure to take the children would have meant abandoning them to the foster care system. For the majority of grandparents, this role comes as a surprise and with little time to plan. Some have had little contact with the child before suddenly becoming the child's caregiver (Cox, 2002). Substance abuse, death (particularly as a result of HIV/AIDS), and incarceration are three main catalysts to grandparents becoming parents. They may be angry and resentful at their fate, at their adult children for putting them in the situation, and for having to exhaust their savings and energy for children with whom they may not have had much contact prior to assuming guardianship. Their stress levels tend to be high, especially since these grandparents are often raising children without spouses or partners (Glass & Huneycutt, 2002).

Grandparents who find themselves as parents again often state how out of place they feel, since they no longer fit with their old set of friends, nor do they feel comfortable with the younger parents of their grandchildren's peers (DeToledo & Brown, 1995). Teachers can be especially helpful by introducing custodial grandparents to each other (being careful to respect confidentiality) and by providing information about grandparent support groups. For example, the American Association of Retired Persons has support group contacts, and online search engines yield numerous Web sites that can provide guidance and information.

Custodial grandparents may also feel unqualified to help their grandchildren with schoolwork and could benefit from having the assistance of tutors (Glass & Huneycutt, 2002). Teachers can allay grandparents' fears and alleviate the burden by offering peer tutors or guidance on how to help children with homework. For example, one grandmother "sent a note to the teacher asking for help understanding what young children did in 'computer lab'" (Smith, Dannison, & Vach-Hasse, 1998, p. 15). Providing detailed information on the child's school day, social interactions, and learning experiences may be necessary, since it is likely that the grandparent's own schooling was quite different from the grandchild's.

Custodial grandparents are also likely to be dealing with challenging children. The majority of children under the care of their grandparents may have been abused or neglected, and many have associated behavioral and emotional problems (Dowdell, 1995). For some of these children, going to school on a daily basis is a new experience and an additional challenge for grandparents to enforce (Glass & Huneycutt, 2002). If mere attendance is unfamiliar, homework and other school-related activities requiring compliance and cooperation may prove even tougher for grandparents to coax.

Role-playing has also been found to be particularly helpful in teaching grandparents how to deal with difficult topics (Cox, 2002). This may include helping grandparents practice how to handle difficult behaviors exhibited by the grandchild, as well as rehearse how to deal with specific events in the special education cycle (e.g., raising concerns at a triennial evaluation). Understanding that custodial grandparents are sacrificing their retirement to assume the demanding role of parenting their grand-children—which includes dealing with everything from psychological problems to legal hassles—is important. Providing custodial grandparents support and expressing appreciation of their efforts can go a long way toward establishing a strong working relationship (Smith et al., 1998).

Secondary Caregivers

Grandparents who are willing and able (i.e., not restricted by advanced age, health, or geographic distance) can be great sources of support for families with children with special needs. As secondary caregivers, they can provide tangible help, such as babysitting and assistance with daily care. Furthermore, grandparents can be a source of emotional support. Assistance from grandparents has been found to contribute to parents' abilities to keep a positive outlook and avoid physical exhaustion (Green, 2001).

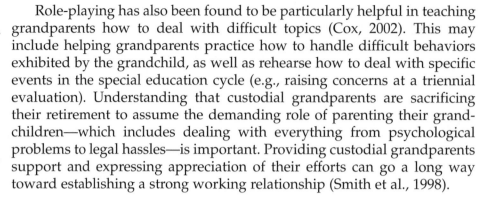

Inquire whether there are extended family members, such as grandparents, who would like to become more involved in the child's schooling.

For example, many parents of children with disabilities report that the grandparents' pride, normalized attitudes toward the child, and uncondi-tional acceptance of the child are especially helpful in their feeling sup-ported (Green, 2001; Seligman & Darling, 1997). One mother was touched by the fact that her parents loved to show friends pictures of her son despite his physical abnormalities, just as any other grandparents would show off to their friends.

It is helpful to inquire whether there are extended family members, such as grandparents, who would like to become more involved in the child's schooling. Reaching out to these secondary caregivers is not only a way to help the child but may relieve a burden from stressed parents, par-ticularly when working with parents who do not participate as much as desired. One way to do this is in your classroom newsletter or a general letter home to all parents, so as not to single out (and thus offend) specific parents. With the parents' permission, these family members may be instructed on how to read with the child or engage in other tasks that rein-force concepts at school. For example, one mother stated that she and her husband were unable to devote the time required to practice their son's gross motor skills at home, but the child's grandmother did: "She would play with my son and make a big game out of things that the therapist wanted him to practice on. I believe because of her and her husband playing with him, he is able to walk today" (Baranowski & Schilmoeller, 1999, p. 441). In addition, grandparents may be able to visit or volunteer during the school day when working parents cannot.

Many grandparents state that they have limited information about their grandchild's disability and are not sure what to expect from their grandchildren (Vadasy, Fewell, & Meyer, 1986). If you have parental permission to involve grandparents who are secondary caregivers, it may be helpful to share information about the child's disability as appropriate. You may also find that grandparents accept the disability more readily than the child's parents, perhaps because there are fewer implications of the disability for the grandparents than for the parents (Hastings, 1997).

Not-So-Secondary Caregivers

Noncustodial grandparents who are serving as de facto parents require special sensitivity. These include grandparents who do not have legal custody but are raising their grandchildren, as well as grandparents who clearly function as the matriarch or patriarch of an extended family. For example, many children reside with one or both of their parents in their grandparents' homes. Often this is a temporary arrangement due to financial difficulties, but it may also last for years.

In one case, a teacher was growing increasingly frustrated by the behavior problems of a 7-year-old boy named Sal. Despite notes home and calls to his mother, little changed. A student study team meeting was convened, and the mother arrived with Sal's aunt and grandmother. It was clear in everyone's demeanor and behavior that the grandmother was in charge of the family. The teacher was surprised to be confronted by the boy's grandmother, who bellowed, "Why didn't anyone tell me Sal was having problems?!" The teacher was tempted to state that the grandmother was not contacted because she was not the parent. Instead, the teacher apologized for not being aware of the need to contact the grandmother, further stating that it was obvious that some headway could be made now that the grandmother was involved. Recognizing the importance and power of the grandmother was crucial to working with this family.

When working with any parent, identify other significant adults in the child's life who should be treated as parents and co-collaborators. This is particularly relevant for cultural groups that emphasize extended kinship networks (e.g., African Americans, Hispanics, American Indians, and Asians). It is estimated that one in three African American families is headed by elderly women (Hill, 1993), possibly because grandparents serve as informal adopters (Mosley-Howard & Evans, 2000). Identifying de facto parents ensures you are being respectful of family dynamics and will be working with the true power brokers. Early in the year, meet with the parents and other significant adults to clarify roles and lines of communication. Ascertain their preferences (e.g., who should be called if there is a behavior problem) and state yours. For example, you may explain that although notes home will be sent to the parent, everyone is welcome at conferences. When you discuss your follow-up meeting, ask whether everyone would like to attend or if it is acceptable to have one representative present, who will later share the information with the others. Being open to these nontraditional arrangements strengthens your relationships with parents and makes them more effective.

> Being open to these nontraditional arrangements strengthens your relationships with parents and makes them more effective.

WORKING WITH NONCUSTODIAL PARENTS

About half of all marriages end in divorce, and nearly one million children experience divorce each year (DeToledo & Brown, 1995). Many of your students reside with one parent, who may be too consumed with other responsibilities to be actively involved in the classroom. But what about the noncustodial parent? Despite their legal status, many noncustodial parents (often fathers) remain important individuals in their children's lives and make efforts to maximize their time with their children. For example,

> Carl worked as a maintenance man in a factory. He worked 6 days a week and had to check the factory on Sunday. He chose to go to work at five o'clock in the morning on Sunday so that he could be home to watch his son play baseball at nine. He never got to visit his son in school because his boss never would give him the time off from work. (Friedman & Berkeley, 2002, p. 210)

Friedman (1998) argues that divorced fathers are an underutilized resource. He states, "Teachers need to recognize that fathers, whether they coreside with their children or not, can be competent parents and should be treated as serious partners in the rearing of their children" (p. 239).

Furthermore, the Family Educational Rights and Privacy Act of 1974, also known as the Buckley Amendment, protects the rights of noncustodial parents to participate in their child's schooling (and inspect records) unless specifically denied those rights by the courts (Jacob & Hartshorne, 1991).

Indeed, many noncustodial parents desire to be more involved with their children, but need an invitation to do so at school, which may be seen as the domain of the custodial parent. Friedman (1998) provides several suggestions for reaching out to divorced fathers, including sending all messages and newsletters to both parents (mailing them to the non-coresiding parent rather than making it the child's burden to distribute it) and giving parents the option to have conferences together or separately. In some cases it may be necessary for teachers to help divorced couples deal with their reluctance to interact with one another. Often, focusing on the child's needs will override parents' tension with one another. For example, one teacher was able to convince a father to attend an event despite his inclination to avoid his former wife by asking him

> what he would do if someone said that either he or his daughter had to take a punch in the stomach. He looked puzzled but replied, "Of course I would take the punch." Ms Binghamton then asked him to take an "emotional punch" from his ex-wife and come to the party because his daughter needed him. (Friedman, 1998, p. 241)

Similar reasoning can be applied to encourage divorced couples to attend conferences together so as not to exhaust your time and resources.

You may also find creative ways to use cassettes or videotapes (e.g., of the child's performance or reading aloud) in addition to letters and e-mail to engage noncustodial parents. Other suggestions for involving noncustodial parents include having flexible times for visiting, allowing them to borrow books, and providing information in your classroom newsletters about low-cost weekend educational activities and good educational toys to aid in gift-giving (Friedman & Berkeley, 2002). Lynda Tripp, a principal in Lynnwood, Washington, suggests asking noncustodial parents to submit 10 legal-sized, self-addressed, stamped envelopes to be used by the school to forward copies of report cards, newsletters, and the like. Numbering the envelopes allows the parent to be alert to when it is time to supply more.

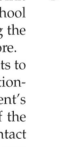

Reaching out to noncustodial parents may bring unexpected benefits to the child and to your classroom, but at the same time impact your relationship with the custodial parent. Being respectful of the custodial parent's wishes is important, and judgment must be exercised. For example, if the mother, as the custodial parent, states that she is trying to limit contact between the child and his father because the father is verbally abusive, you may not want to invite the father to be a classroom volunteer. However, you can inquire whether it would be acceptable to send duplicate notes home about the child's progress or to involve him in conferences.

WORKING WITH FOSTER PARENTS

Foster parents are a diverse group, ranging in their motivations for taking in children, their commitment to their foster children, their understanding

Table 7.1 **Main Points for Working With Nontraditional Families**
1. Assist grandparents by providing specific information and encouragement
2. Involve noncustodial parents as much as possible
3. Support foster parents in their role as surrogate parents
4. Keep reasonable expectations for homeless parents
5. Consider whether you should inform parents of your child abuse/neglect report

of child development, their parenting styles, and their views of their roles as caregivers. The media typically depict only two types of foster parents—those who are "saints" caring for multiple foster children, particularly children with disabilities, and those who are abusive, such as the father who reportedly killed his 10-year-old foster daughter as a result of severe corporal punishment (Baker, 2003). Clearly, these are the extremes, and the majority of foster parents fall somewhere in between.

Unfortunately, not all foster parents are exceptionally altruistic or suited to parenting. Paula McLain was 4 years old when she and her siblings were placed in foster care and spent 14 years in and out of people's homes. She recounts that one foster father "was old enough to be our grandfather [but] wasn't grandfatherly at all. He was creepy and lascivious." She wonders "if some of our foster parents took us in just for the checks" (McLain, 2002, p. 124). Although there is no published data to support it, anecdotal evidence suggests that some families' motivation for becoming foster parents is the extra income (up to $1200/month in some states).

While the majority of foster parents view their role as parent or substitute parent (Orme & Buehler, 2001), some do not. Research suggests that approximately 15–20% of foster parents exhibit significant problems in home environment, family functioning, and parenting (Orme & Buehler). This may include excessive physical punishment, low empathy toward children's needs, inappropriate developmental expectations and problematic attitudes toward parent–child roles as well as psychiatric problems in the foster parents (Campbell, Simon, Weithorn, Krikston, & Connolly, 1980; Gaudin & Sutphen, 1993). For example, one study found 21% of foster homes had parents who engaged in no or minimal interactions with the foster children during the interview, despite interviewer requests for such interactions (Simms & Horwitz, 1996). As a result, it behooves teachers to give information about child development and to help foster parents have realistic expectations for their foster children, particularly children with special needs.

Although states vary in their requirements, training to become a foster parent typically includes little information about working with the education system. For example, the state of North Carolina requires 30 hours of training before individuals can be licensed as foster parents. Topics include communication skills, separation and loss, behavior management, working with birth families, and the impact of placement on foster families. In addition, 10 hours of training annually are required to maintain a license. Nonetheless, "one of the most prevalent concerns among foster families over the years has been that they have not felt prepared to face the challenges presented by children in foster care" (Hunt & West, 1997). Many teachers may expect too much of foster parents, assuming they are trained and knowledgeable in all areas of childrearing. It may be necessary to educate foster parents about the special education system, about their roles as active participants, and about the benefits of parent–teacher collaboration. Still, some foster parents may be consumed with other issues of their foster children, such as medical needs and therapy appointments, and may have limited time and energy to devote to children's education. One foster mother felt her duties were fulfilled by meeting the basic physical needs of her 8-year-old foster son and left everything else up to the boy's social worker. In this case, the social worker tried to be involved with the boy's educational and counseling needs but often lacked the time to follow through.

Rather than focusing on what foster parents can do for you, it may be necessary to look to what you, as a teacher, can do. Summarizing research about foster parents' satisfaction and intent to foster, Denby, Rindfleisch, and Bean (1999) state, "Perhaps just giving foster parents any amount of special attention motivates them to persevere as providers" (p. 290). Providing support, encouragement, and appreciation can boost foster parents' coping. This has implications not just for your relationships with foster parents, but also for the children they care for. Your support may mean that the foster parents choose to endure difficult child behaviors (e.g., sexual acting out) and continue caring for the child, rather than asking to have the child placed with another family. This encouragement is especially important for foster parents of children with special needs, who are typically difficult to place (Orme & Buehler, 2001).

WORKING WITH HOMELESS FAMILIES

Homeless families are by nature transient, and you may have only a very short time period in which to make an impact. Children in homeless families especially need structure and security, which a caring teacher and classroom can provide. Although you may not be able to develop the textbook ideal working relationship with parents of homeless children, creating a strong rapport can pave the way for effective collaboration. Swick

(1999) suggests four steps to developing partnerships with homeless and highly transient parents:

> The first step is the building of a trusting relationship through nurturing and respectful visits and conferences. . . . Second, involve parents in being partners in helping their children become educationally competent. . . . Third, involve them in their children's education at school. . . . Fourth, engage parents in increasing their own educational skills. (pp. 197–198)

By being caring, being supportive, and providing guidance about how parents can teach their children, teachers can make a significant difference in the lives of homeless children.

Being a homeless parent's ally may mean being a liaison with other services as well as being their advocate (e.g., mobilizing school resources to help the family). For example, one teacher reflected:

> I did not know Ben was homeless but I did know that he was not involved in any school functions, and often his homework was turned in on very crumpled paper. I began to spend time with him after school—tutoring him in some subjects and being a friend. When I drove him home he told me in a real quiet voice "We live at the shelter until my mom can find a place."

> I got him involved at school, had the coach waive the fees for basketball and linked him up with two boys who I knew would be a good influence. I have also visited his mother at the shelter and the two of us are encouraging Ben to keep up with schoolwork. It is making a difference—he is thriving and finding ways to be someone positive in this world. (Swick, 1999, p. 197)

Being sympathetic and nonjudgmental may reap immediate results or it may inspire parents to be more involved at a later date, when their life circumstances stabilize. No parent wants to be homeless, nor do they want to be treated as if they are irresponsible and reprehensible. Meet them where they are (i.e., they are doing the best they can), and encourage them to unite with you to help their child.

Keep your expectations—of the child and parents—reasonable. For instance, many homeless children do not have a quiet place to do their homework. Swick (1999)

> **Being sympathetic and nonjudgmental may reap immediate results or it may inspire parents to be more involved at a later date, when their life circumstances stabilize.**

states, "The educational priorities of . . . teachers may need to be postponed until critical survival needs are addressed" (p. 196). Convey this understanding in your attitude toward homeless parents so as not to alienate them by making more demands than they can fulfill. Nevertheless, parents can be encouraged to help their children learn in small manageable ways, such as by reinforcing basic skills (e.g., reciting multiplication facts or spelling words while waiting in line or reading street signs together).

> "The educational priorities of . . . teachers may need to be postponed until critical survival needs are addressed."

Although these parents may be consumed with immediate needs of food, clothing, and shelter, they are no less desiring of the knowledge that their children are liked and cared for. These parents in particular may benefit from a note home acknowledging the child's strengths or accomplishments and a special invitation to meet with you. Waiting for quarterly parent conferences may be unwise, since they may no longer be in your school at that point. Instead, as soon as you are able to offer any insights about the student or can identify any short-term goals, invite parents for a meeting. Keep in mind that transportation may present a hardship and be creative in your problem solving (e.g., does the school have any discretionary funds for bus tokens or are other parents willing to carpool?). You may need to arrange a telephone call instead, though this is less desirable than face-to-face interaction. Also, childcare may be a concern. You may need to assure the parent that he or she can bring children to the meeting and provide a quiet activity for them to do.

If you can, provide something tangible. For example, if you want to encourage parents to read to their child, give them an appropriate book or children's magazine as well as suggestions on how to make the most of their five minutes of reading together. Many homeless children do not have basic supplies such as paper and pencils. At the same time, be sure to praise parents for their achievements (Swick, 1999). Rather than focusing on all of the things they have not been able to do with their child, heap attention and praise on the one area they have succeeded in, even if it is as basic as attendance and lack of tardiness (the bus may bring them to school, but the parents still make sure the child gets on the bus). Also, consider making a portfolio for the child, which depicts his or her skills well. This may be especially useful when the child changes schools.

Homeless parents may feel powerless, but they still have something to offer. You can invite them to participate (e.g., they can lead the class in a sing-along of the child's favorite songs or demonstrate how to cook a child's favorite dish), but be gracious and understanding about their apparent non-involvement. They may have personal reasons (e.g., embarrassment) that prevent them from volunteering or may have legitimate concerns (e.g., the need to care for other children) that keep them away. You can remind them—or educate them—about their importance and that they have much to give their children despite their dire financial conditions.

WORKING WITH FAMILIES WHERE YOU SUSPECT CHILD ABUSE OR NEGLECT

Being a mandated reporter for suspicion of child abuse or neglect is a profound responsibility, one that many teachers are apprehensive about. Many teachers may think a child is being abused or neglected, but are reluctant to report, because they do not have enough information, do not want to pass judgment on a family, or do not want to make waves. Indeed, in one study by the National Center on Child Abuse and Neglect, almost 40% of mandated reporters admitted to suspecting abuse but failing to report it (Zellman & Bell, 1990). Whether the signs of abuse are scant or impossible to ignore, teachers have a legal obligation to make a report when abuse and neglect are suspected. Erring on the side of reporting ensures that you provide the opportunity for an abused child to receive help. Shirking the duty to report may further isolate the child whose abuse is being ignored by the adults around him or her.

When faced with a situation in which you suspect abuse or neglect, most people experience a range of emotions. These include anger at the suspected perpetrator, dismay and compassion for the child, stress regarding your role, and guilt and fear regarding the report (Nunnelley & Fields, 1999). Some schools have a centralized reporting system, having one person (e.g., the social worker or counselor) make all reports, while others leave it up to the individual professional.

Whether you call the child welfare authorities (e.g., Child Protective Services [CPS]; these designations vary by state) to make the report or provide the information so another person can do it, your anxiety may be focused on two issues: Is this really what is best for the child? What if the parent figures out I reported him or her? Both questions are valid, since the outcome of the report cannot be predicted. Although not all reports are acted upon (or even accepted), those that are may result in outcomes ranging from a one-time investigation to removal of the children and placement in foster care. Many parents are able to trace the reporter based on the information in the report (e.g., "told someone at school his father beat him"). Parents may become suspicious of all school staff as a result. In some cases, the investigating worker may inform the parents of the source, either intentionally to validate the claim or accidentally. If this is the case, parents typically become resentful of the teacher and school (though few will take serious action), and any opportunity for collaboration is generally lost. For example, one irate mother recounted, "They did not say anything and they called me up to say they were bringing somebody from school to enroll John in a school but it was nobody from a school, it was child abuse. They never told me this" (Rao, 2000, p. 480). Following the incident, this mother began to question her initial decision to seek help for her son.

How should teachers handle their responsibility to report suspected abuse and neglect? There is no one correct response, and the extent to which teachers should be involved with these families remains controversial.

First and foremost, know the child abuse laws in your state well. Keep a copy of them in your classroom. When school policies conflict with the law, abide by the law in all instances, since it is the law (not school policies) that will protect you. Similarly, know the general investigative procedures used by the child welfare agency in your state, such as whether you can call for a consultation, time frames for investigation, and so forth.

Second, it is imperative to seek help and counsel from other professionals. Do not feel you have to bear the responsibility by yourself, even if your school policy requires that you make the report. Inform the principal and other staff members as appropriate (e.g., the school psychologist or counselor who may be involved with the child), not only so you can be assisted and feel supported, but also so they can present a united front to an upset parent. Should you encounter an administrator who pressures you into dropping the issue, it is all the more important to seek out others who can help you fulfill your legal obligation.

Third, consider the situation and exercise judgment accordingly. If the family is clearly known to have a history of violence or substance abuse, is exceptionally chaotic, or is completely unknown to you and your colleagues (e.g., new to the school), it may be best to make an anonymous report to child welfare and take no further action. This is also true if you have a contentious relationship with the family.

If, however, you know the family to be reasonable or have developed a positive relationship with the family, consider contacting them in addition to making the report. The mere suggestion that you should talk directly with families you need to report raises anxiety in many teachers. Many would argue that contact with the family is best left to the authorities. Unfortunately, this leaves you no control over how the report will be presented to the parents and what information will be given. It is all too easy for someone else, including a well-intentioned colleague, to backpedal when confronted by a parent (e.g., "I'm just telling you what the teacher thinks."). For example, one teacher shared that a social worker informed the family that she and the teacher suspected abuse and reported it, only to have it backfire.

Though it may seem ludicrous, informing the family that you have had to (or are about to) make a report is a vital step to maintaining a positive relationship with the parents. Doing so allows you (not someone else) to frame the report in a compassionate manner, explaining that you do not intend to get them in trouble, but are focused on the welfare of the child.

Surprisingly, many parents are receptive and appreciative when informed in advance about a child abuse report. In your conversation with the parent, provide basic information about why the report was made, but do not dwell on it. Stating the child has bruises is enough; you do not have to detail all of your other suspicions. Instead, focus on your response as a caring teacher.

Ideally, you would speak to the parent (probably by phone because of the time frame of the report), rather than send a letter. Inform the parent of the reason for the report, any action child welfare may take (e.g., they may tell you when you file the phone report that they will investigate within 10 days), and what your response is. Offer support, remind the parent of your desire to help him or her and the child, and leave the door open for future contact.

Consider the scenario where over a period of time you begin to suspect a student is being abused at home, possibly by his parents. When you call the parents, you might frame the report in the following manner:

> You probably know that teachers are required to report any suspicions of child abuse or neglect and that we really don't have any choice about it. We just have to inform Child Protective Services if there are any signs of possible abuse or neglect, and they are the ones who investigate what's happening. So today, Stephen came to school with a lot of bruises and he told someone that he had been beaten at home. That's the kind of thing we have to report. I had to call CPS and tell them what Stephen said, and CPS said they will probably come out to your house to investigate, but they didn't tell me when.

> I wanted to tell you personally, because I want to make sure you know that I am not judging you or trying to get you in trouble. I made the report because I am required to, but also because I really care about Stephen, and if there are special services the state can provide for him, like counseling, I want you to get them. Does that make sense?

Allow the parent to respond to what you have said. If the parent gives you excuses for what you see as signs of abuse (e.g., "He just fell off his bike again."), you can accept them graciously (e.g., "Oh, how terrible!"), and remind the parent that you are not investigating, merely reporting (e.g., "Unfortunately, bruises is on the list of things we have to report."). Clarify any issues, which may include reassuring them about information given (e.g., "I just told CPS Stephen had bruises and told someone about being beaten, that's it.") and providing them with basic information about the child welfare laws in your state (e.g., "I know they can get families respite care, which is like free babysitting, and counseling.").

End the conversation by offering your assistance and appreciation. For example, you can say, "I really appreciate your being so understanding about all of this. Stephen is really a great kid—he can be so funny sometimes. Let me know if there is anything I can do to help." Do not seek reassurance from the parent, such as by saying, "I hope you aren't mad at me for making the report." Seeking such a response projects a less-than-professional image, and the fact is that making a report is one of your professional duties, just like giving a child a failing grade.

Talking with parents about child abuse reports in this manner does not ensure they will respond positively, but it does reduce the possibility of parents feeling betrayed. Being open and honest also prevents the dark secret of abuse from clouding your relationship with the family. It may also pave the way for collaboration, by allowing parents to disclose their struggles (e.g., "Did you say something about counseling? I'm going crazy with Stephen—he really needs some help."), which in turn enables you to join with them to help the child. You may also be able to offer information on outside resources, such as Parents Anonymous, a nationwide organization that assists parents who fear they may abuse their child. Incidentally, informing the parents also gives them a chance to deal with their emotions before the child abuse worker meets them. While this may be unpleasant for you, it may raise the possibility that the parents will be more receptive to what the worker says.

As a final note, remember that once your report is made, "it is in the classroom that teachers . . . have the greatest opportunity for making a positive difference in the lives of abused and neglected children" (Barrett-Kruse, Martinez, & Carll, 1998, p. 60). Addressing children's learning deficits, building their self-esteem and relationship skills, and empowering them by focusing on their strengths are unequivocally helpful.

REFLECTING ON YOUR TEACHING

When discussing parent involvement, it is easy to think in terms of traditional families and to overlook others. Use the following questions and activities to reflect on your own teaching and broaden your approaches to working with nontraditional families.

1. Identify any students who are being raised by grandparents and consider ways you can support them.

2. How could you involve noncustodial parents in their children's education?

3. Are you aware of any of your students being in foster care? If so, consider contacting the foster parent and social worker regarding ways you can help and what involvement you would like from them.

4. What attitudes and beliefs do you have about homelessness? How might these impact your interactions with homeless parents?

5. Compile an activity bag or resource bag to provide to homeless families, noncustodial parents, or grandparents who may need them. The bag may contain instructions for a joint activity with the student and supplies, as well as information on child development, community resources, and school supports.

6. Obtain a copy of the child abuse laws and review it. Research your school policies regarding mandated reporting.

SUMMARY

Teachers may encounter particular populations, such as grandparents, noncustodial parents, foster parents, and homeless families, who require sensitivity and specific approaches in order to build collaborative relationships. These may include providing information on child development and educational needs, guiding parents to appropriate resources, making special efforts to involve parents, and being supportive and empathic. With some families, you might consider making a child abuse report in an open manner with a frank discussion with the parents to increase the possibility that you will be able to maintain a positive working relationship with the family.

CULTIVATING
COLLABORATIVE
RELATIONSHIPS

"Good teachers, no matter where they teach and live, share similar qualities. . . . They delight in our children's successes and challenges. They help them, and us, deal with our issues. . . . They reach out to our children and to us, knowing that parental involvement makes all the difference in whether children learn and enjoy school."

Susan Bernard
Parent and Author of *The Mommy and Daddy Guide to Kindergarten* (2001, p. 3)

I t's a common complaint, one that both novice and seasoned teachers have been heard to utter—"It's not the kids who make my job hard, it's the parents!" When you first started teaching, however, every aspect of teaching was challenging, from learning how to work the mimeograph machine to tailoring reading lessons for a student with learning disabilities. Over time (and a lot of hard work), working with children became second nature. Similarly, initially it may seem like an inordinate amount of time and effort is required to build collaborative relationships with parents. However, being conscientious in your relationships with parents will reap like rewards, and working with parents will also become second nature.

Cultivating collaborative relationships with parents is different than enlisting them to be classroom helpers, though that may be a role some choose to adopt. In collaboration, both you and the parents are "compelled by . . . shared responsibility for the outcome . . . neither party is free. Each is equally tied to the well-being" of the child (Caplan & Caplan, 1993, p. 282). This type of relationship is not only deliberately created, but a mind-set. As described in the opening chapter of this book, effective teacher–parent collaboration requires a solid working relationship. This is generally characterized by mutual respect, a clear understanding of roles, similar expectations, defined common goals, opportunities for feedback, and openness to adjustment as needed. But how does this type of relationship happen? It is helpful to conceptualize collaborative relationships with parents as evolving through three stages. Keep in mind, however, that these stages are fluid and that the type of relationship that is most desired by parents and professionals is "a process that evolves much like a friendship: using conversation and mutual self-disclosure, avoiding formal measures of any kind, and proceeding at a pace that is unhurried and with an attitude that is nonjudgmental, supportive and caring" (Summers et al., 1990, p. 97).

The first stage is focused on building credibility and establishing yourself as a caring competent professional who is able to work with the parents' child. In addition to motivating parents to desire collaboration, you will also define roles for both you and the parent. The middle phase hinges upon good communication and the ability to effectively resolve conflicts. In the final stage, termination, deliberateness in your relationship will encourage future cooperation with other teachers and parents.

Before you begin, however, it is important to be aware of personal and cultural issues that may affect your relationships with parents.

RESOLVING YOUR RESERVATIONS

Time pressures, inadequate training, a lack of institutional support, and insufficient resources may all be valid reasons for shying away from stronger relationships with parents. Yet it is another hesitation that may really keep you from collaboration—your personal discomfort. Some teachers feel the need to assert control over their classrooms and see parent involvement as a threat to or challenge of their control (Lewis & Forman, 2002). Indeed, some teachers have admitted that one of the main concerns they have regarding parent involvement is that parents will judge them. As one educator stated,

> I can remember the first time I was asked to invite parents to be volunteers in my classroom. Real feelings of anxiety stirred within me. Would the parents be there to judge and evaluate me? What if I did something they did not like or understand? Could I teach comfortably with another adult in my classroom? (Hurt, 2000, p. 88)

Others have said, "If I have a parent in my classroom, I feel like I'm on display," and "What if they think I'm a bad teacher?"

Overcoming these anxieties, not unlike those you may have experienced when you first started teaching, is important. Yes, some parents will judge you, and some will question what they see in your classroom. The majority of parents, however, will be focused on their child, not you, and will be happy to be involved. (Providing parents with an observation sheet such as the one found in Resource E further increases the likelihood that they will focus on their child rather than dissect you.) Be assured that effective teaching methods will stand the test of parents' questions and criticism (Cutler, 1993). Furthermore, parents who are involved tend to have an increased appreciation for teachers' skills and abilities (Epstein, 2000). Specifically, parents tend to rate teachers higher in overall teaching ability and interpersonal skills if they frequently encourage parent involvement (Epstein, 1986). As when you were a new teacher, you will find your comfort level with parents increases as you gain experience.

Another concern that may hold you back is the feeling that asking for help from parents or treating them as equals means admitting professional failure or shortcomings. It is helpful if your school's culture views the educational process as a joint undertaking, where everyone (teachers included) is learning and growing (Lewis & Forman, 2002). If your school (or you) expects perfection from teachers, it will be difficult to convince yourself that you can partner equally with parents. Remember that collaborative relationships involve equals:

> All parties are perceived as possessing important knowledge and skills, and it is assumed that parents and teachers will be willing to share information, learn from each other, value each other's input, and incorporate each other's insights into programmatic considerations. Pooling information, sharing resources of the home and the school, obtaining clearer conceptualizations of problems, and

increasing the range and superiority of solutions are primary goals. (Sheridan & Kratochwill, 1992, p. 123–124)

Neither the parent nor you are expected to be all knowing; both of you have skills and traits that benefit the partnership.

In the end, you may still have some reservations about collaborating with parents. While these should be heeded to some extent—you should know your own limits as well as strengths and weaknesses—they need not prevent you from entering into potentially beneficial relationships with parents.

APPLYING CULTURAL CONSIDERATIONS

Research has found that "when teachers differ culturally and educationally from their students . . . they are less likely to know the students' parents and therefore, more likely to believe that parents are disinterested or uninvolved" (Epstein & Dauber, 1991, p. 298). The overall assumption in the past was that families should accommodate the school's value system rather than the school accommodating specific populations (Hoover-Dempsey & Sandler, 1995).

> Teachers who are skilled in working with diverse populations are more effective educators and collaborators.

Yet in today's increasingly diverse society, sensitivity to families' views of education is prudent. Teachers who are skilled in working with diverse populations are more effective educators and collaborators. Divergent values, attitudes, child-rearing practices, and communication patterns all affect your relationships with parents from culturally and linguistically diverse groups. For example, Quiroz, Greenfield, and Altchech (1999) state, "In the interdependent perspective of Latino immigrant parents, education is a tool not for developing the *individual* potential of each child, but for enabling each child to *help the family as a whole*" (p. 68, emphasis added).

As a teacher, you may struggle to reconcile the cultural differences between you and your students' parents. "The issue is not that professionals should change their own beliefs, but that they must learn ways of understanding and respecting the beliefs of the families they work with" (Harry, 2002, p. 135). It is helpful to be aware of your own attitudes toward persons from other cultures as well as to have an understanding of other cultures (Jordan, Reyes-Blanes, Peel, Peel, & Lane, 1998). For example, your training and background may lead you to expect that parent conferences should involve the parent(s) and the teacher only, while in African American or Latino cultures, it would be appropriate for parents and significant extended family members to participate (Jordan et al.).

In addition, making efforts to learn about your students' backgrounds and incorporating them into the school program is helpful for building collaborative relationships with parents. This may be as simple as wishing a Vietnamese family a happy new year during the Vietnamese New Year celebration (Flett & Conderman, 2001) or incorporating poems from the students' home countries in your poetry unit. Parents will feel more invested in their roles as partners in education if they feel their culture is welcomed into the classroom. Parents can be encouraged to share their child's favorite stories, music, or food; family photographs of cultural activities can also be used on bulletin boards or in class newsletters.

Understanding how different cultural and ethnic groups view disabilities is also useful. For example, many Chinese parents tend to attribute academic achievement more to effort than to innate ability (Schneider & Lee, 1990) and may hold the same expectations for a child with learning disabilities as for a child without disabilities. Many African American families view placement in a special education program as temporary, until the child "catches up" (Harry et al., 1995). "It is important to recognize that parents and their children with disabilities do have a vision; finding a way to support them through their journey toward that vision would help in building more meaningful partnerships with families" (Rao, 2000, p. 486).

Sensitivity to parents' experiences of formal schooling is also important. For example, some immigrant parents who had limited educational opportunities in their homeland may struggle to teach their children to be students (Hayes, 1992). This lack of preparation includes tangible behaviors such as how to research and write a report as well as intangibles such as showing initiative in the classroom. Whether families are voluntary immigrants who may have come to the United States in search of opportunity (e.g., Asian Americans and Mexican immigrants) or involuntary immigrants who have suffered slavery or colonization (e.g., African Americans, Native Americans) also impacts families' experiences in formal schooling (Hayes).

In addition, demonstrating cultural sensitivity means accommodating families for whom English is not the primary language. Having an interpreter present for your communications with parents, both formal and informal, is essential. Parents who speak English on a functional level may still prefer to have formal letters from school translated (Flett & Conderman, 2001). If at all possible, avoid using the child as the interpreter, even if the parents turn to the child for language assistance. Jordan et al. (1998) state that using the student as the interpreter "distorts the roles of parent and child," making it inappropriate for diverse groups (p. 144). In addition, using the student as the interpreter may negatively impact the communication due to the child's language proficiency and self-censorship by you and the parent. You may also want to encourage two or more parents who speak the same language to volunteer together to increase their comfort and confidence in the classroom (Flett & Conderman).

At the same time, it is important to remember that families' varying levels of acculturation and adherence to cultural norms means that you need to treat each family uniquely. Rather than making assumptions about a family based on its language or culture, endeavor to get to know the unique perspective of the parents. Explicitly addressing cultural differences enables finding common ground.

STARTING AT THE BEGINNING

As the saying goes, "You don't get a second chance to make a first impression." It is better to devote particular attention at the outset of the relationship to promote cooperation than to try to salvage a relationship that began poorly. In a romantic relationship, you would not ask someone to clean your toilets on your first date. By the same token, jumping right into the meat of a working relationship with parents, such as by making your first interaction a meeting to discuss a child's behavior problems, sets the relationship up for failure. Making your initial contact with parents positive is essential. One school encouraged its teachers to contact all 160 parents within the first two weeks of school (Ramirez, 2001). While this may sound daunting, it is feasible to make brief phone calls or send e-mails to introduce yourself and invite the parent to participate. You can also send a Back-to-School letter, similar to the sample in Resource F, to encourage contact with you and to get information about parents.

> Explicitly addressing cultural differences enables finding common ground.

Building Credibility

When entering into any working relationship, be it a doctor with a patient, a teacher with a parent, or a plumber with a homeowner, the first order of business is to establish credibility. By nature of your title and formal role of educator, you already have some credibility as an expert. Most parents expect that you are more skilled than they are in educating children. Being organized, efficient, skilled in classroom management, and in calm command of your classroom further reinforces your expert credibility. For example, at Back-to-School Night, have a polished presentation for parents with handouts. "Parents will assume you conduct your presentation in the same way you teach your class" (Ribas, 1998).

In addition, however, you need to establish credibility as the educator of the parents' child. This means conveying to parents that you know and understand their child, have positive attitudes toward and expectations of their child, and recognize the strengths (not just the weaknesses) of their particular child. Teachers naturally have a group orientation, whereas parents naturally have an individualistic orientation (i.e., they are thinking about the well-being of their child, not the 25 other children in the classroom). When talking with parents, it is helpful to frame things toward the individual (e.g., "Jonelle is learning fractions now")

> You need to establish credibility as the educator of the parents' child.

rather than discussing learning in terms of the group (e.g., "The class is learning fractions.") Show parents that you know the child as an individual by recounting specific comments the child made or by noting specific progress in a nonacademic matter (e.g., making a new friend). At the same time, remember that your objective perspective as a teacher may clash with parents' subjective view of their child, and be respectful of parents' protective urges (Lytle & Bordin, 2001).

With parents of students with special needs, you may also need to establish your credibility with regard to the child's disabilities. You may have a solid understanding of how to work with children who have developmental, learning, or emotional and behavioral problems, but no one can be an expert in all things. For example, if a father informs you that his son has neurofibromitosis, and you are unsure of the educational implications of this condition, be honest. Share what you do know about children whose medical conditions are associated with learning problems and about effective ways to teach children with chronic medical illnesses. At the same time, state that you would like more information about the child's disorder or are working with the occupational therapist about how to address the child's disabilities.

Using Helpful Interpersonal Skills

Research with parents of special needs children is generally consistent in its findings regarding what interpersonal skills parents feel are helpful to collaboration. These include (Dinnebeil, Hale, & Rule, 1996)

Friendliness

Optimism

Patience

Sincerity and honesty

Tact

Responsiveness

Openness to suggestions

In addition, respect for parents' decisions has also been cited by parents as helping collaboration, and its absence is harmful (Dinnebeil et al., 1996). Specifically, an attitude of superiority or giving the impression that the teacher's way is the only way hinders collaboration. Rather, collaboration is improved when parents and teachers are viewed as equal partners. Including parents in decision making and using parents' ideas is evidence of this equal partnership. Educators who are flexible, such as in scheduling appointments around parents' work hours and children's needs, are also seen as enhancing collaboration (Dinnebeil, Hale, & Rule, 1999).

Motivating Parents

Research on successful coalitions has found that "coalitions are more likely to succeed when the motivation for the coalition comes from within the community" (Wolff, 2001, p. 174). If the collaboration feels imposed, parents may pull back or rebel. Inquire about parents' past experiences working with their child's teachers, particularly if you sense that they do not share your desire for a close working relationship. Perhaps they were burned by a previous relationship or perhaps they have never been asked directly to be involved.

Central to motivating parents to desire collaboration is an understanding of their concerns and goals. While you as a teacher may be concerned with maximizing student potential and educating for future success, some parents may be more occupied with "getting by" or "keeping my kid out of trouble." Identifying common goals means being flexible (at first on your part and later for the parents). Consider one frustrated mother's tirade:

> I used to spend two or three hours every night on homework with Devin—he has ADHD. It was terrible. Now, I just set the timer—five minutes a page. If he doesn't get it in five minutes, that's it, next page. I told his teacher, "You can't penalize him; he did work on his homework." He has ADHD; it's not fair to penalize him.

This mother was more concerned (at the time) with the daily battles between her and her son, the friction it caused in their family, and the negative attitudes her son was developing toward school, than she was with his skill acquisition. Being flexible and motivating this mother to work with you may start with brainstorming solutions for helping Devin with his homework. Although your preference may be that the mother learns more effective ways to work with her son, you might have to settle for helping Devin get started on his homework after school (and having the parent observe you). Incidentally, you may need to inform the parent of accommodations that can be made in a 504 plan for students with ADHD.

Other parents may not seem particularly interested in being actively involved academically but may express curiosity in "what my child does all day" or in some particular aspect of the school day. Invite parents to observe in the classroom, which can increase their interest in and comfort level with being more actively involved. You can slowly increase your invitation, such as by asking parents if they would like to stay longer to read a book to a few students or to the class. Meeting parents at their levels of interest, rather than imposing expectations of what it means to be involved, is important for motivating parents to be collaborators.

Defining Roles

Many parents need to be informed about the school's expectations for their participation. In particular, the two main expectations and provisions of IDEA regarding parental involvement are equity and advocacy (Kalyanpur, Harry, & Skrtic, 2000). The equity expectation assumes that parents will be equal partners with educators in ensuring an appropriate education for their children. The advocacy expectation assumes that parents will "choose to participate in the decision-making process, make their service preferences known, and seek redress if these requests are not responded to" (Kalyanpur et al., p. 122). Although parents of students with special needs may read about this in the "Introduction to Special Education" literature they are given at their child's entry into the special education system, many are unlikely to grasp the meaning until they are faced with having to exercise their rights. Initially, parents with limited English, of different national origin or backgrounds, or of low socioeconomic status may not feel comfortable being as actively involved as IDEA requires them to be. In your role as the child's teacher, you have the unique opportunity to support and guide parents as they grow into these roles.

In every parent–teacher relationship, roles must be defined for each of you. Fitzgerald and Göncü (1993) have applied Vygotsky's theories of the zone of proximal development to the subject of parent–teacher collaboration. They suggest that just as children learn in a joint activity with a competent partner, adults should explicitly share the skills and information each needs to succeed in their respective domains of home and school. Serpell (1994) states that the first step is to acknowledge and articulate differences in perspective in order to find a common ground. This includes acknowledging cultural differences in values and practices (Kalyanpur & Harry, 1997).

In addition to defining the roles that you and the parents will play, inform parents of the roles of other professionals who are involved with their children. One study found that almost 40% of parents of special education students stated they did not know whether to contact the general or special educator regarding their child's homework (Munk et al., 2001). Having a handout describing the general responsibilities of parents and school professionals (such as the general educator, special educator, school psychologist, and school administrator) may be helpful. Resource G provides an example of how this may be done.

MAINTAINING THE RELATIONSHIP

Communication is at the heart of successful collaboration. Both teachers and parents often feel their communication is inadequate. Unfortunately, each group believes the other party is responsible for not initiating dialogue or more frequent communication (Munk et al., 2001). One parent commented,

> I think it's good for, you know, the parents to be there for their children. He really do like it. It makes me feel closer, but it all depends on the teacher and how they talk to you. If we didn't communicate, I wouldn't come. (Maiers & Nistler, 1998, p. 228)

Although communication is a two-way street, teachers, by virtue of their position alone, bear the responsibility for *initiating* communication.

Some parents and teachers have found that a logbook or journal facilitates regular communication, and e-mail makes this method even simpler (Lytle & Bordin, 2001). Classroom newsletters can be effective tools for encouraging communication. Information sheets explaining common classroom practices are also helpful. These can be created by you or can be printed from other sources (e.g., Web sites), though you need to be mindful of copyrights. For example, you can have handouts on process writing, your classroom management strategies, guidelines for class trip chaperones, and so forth. Just as with other teaching materials, the initial effort put into creating them is outweighed by the benefits of years of use.

Special efforts, such as offering to audio- or videotape the student during the school day, may be especially appreciated by parents (Lytle & Bordin, 2001). Enlisting an instructional aide or parent volunteer makes this a feasible activity. However, informing parents of what is happening in the classroom and specifically with their child is only half of the equation. The other half is listening to parents.

Holding Parent–Teacher Conferences

Your school may use the traditional parent–teacher conference format, may have shifted to student-led conferences, or may even employ group conferences. All three styles, when used effectively, can strengthen parent–teacher collaboration. It is important to consider whether the format of your parent–teacher conferences is culturally compatible with the parents you wish to engage. For example, Quiroz et al. (1999) state that the student-led conference is incompatible with Latino culture because it "violates the collectivistic cultural value in which children respect and look up to their parents as authority figures" (p. 69). In contrast, group conferences are culturally compatible for Latino parents, particularly if translation is provided, such as by a paraprofessional. Quiroz et al. describe how one teacher divided children into ability levels and used group conferences to share information on test score interpretations, report cards, and expectations for the next quarter. When the group session was over, children escorted their parents and siblings to their desks to share their portfolios. Parents then had the option of signing up for a private conference. This format impressed the parents, who saw the teacher's ability to coordinate the group as evidence of her sensitivity to cultural norms and skills as an educator.

Although typically thought of as a forum for giving information to parents, parent–teacher conferences can be used as a means of *listening* to parents. Information on the child's academics as well as social and emotional information can and should be shared by both sides (Lewis & Forman, 2002). Initially, simply inquiring about the student's daily or weekly routine can yield a great deal of pertinent information about the family's values and the child's environment. For example, Ivan Chan, a first-grader, has a regular daily schedule that centers around a Chinese adult world made up mostly of family members:

> [Ivan's] grandmother waits with him in the morning at the school bus stop at the street corner and meets him in the same place in the afternoon. His father may take Ivan to school on his day off. After returning home at 3:45 P.M., Ivan is expected to sit down at a child-sized desk to do homework, which takes 10–15 minutes. There are two kinds of homework: that sent home by the teacher and extra work assigned by Mrs. Chan. After finishing his homework, Ivan can eat a snack and watch television. . . . Sometimes he does activity books and listens to audiocassettes. He also plays with his dog. He is not permitted to go outside to play with children in the neighborhood or visit school friends in their homes. Ivan has no household chores. When Mrs. Chan comes home from work around 6 or 7 P.M., she checks Ivan's work and asks Ivan to make corrections. After supper, the grandmother watches Cantonese television programs beamed from Los Angeles. Ivan sometimes watches these Chinese programs too, especially Chinese martial arts movies. His bedtime is about 9 P.M. (Siu, 1994, p. 25)

Beginning with this information, Ivan's teacher might learn the following:

His parents value and stress education and personal discipline

They are involved on a daily basis at home despite their demanding work schedules

They believe Ivan's responsibility is to study, just as they have their respective work responsibilities

They have concerns about exposing Ivan to undesirable social influences

This understanding will foster collaboration with Ivan's parents, who have high expectations and feel they need to compensate for laxity on the part of the school.

Parent–teacher conferences can be a place for sharing a joint agenda, but this may require parent preparation. Kristi Morris, an educator with 16 years experience, states,

> I always ask the parent ahead of time to be thinking of 2 or 3 things that they would like to see us work on at school with their child. If it was an IEP meeting, I asked the parent to come with what they would like to see their child accomplish in my class.

Approaching parent conferences with the attitude of eliciting valuable input from parents may yield surprising information. Morris adds,

> One time I had a boy who struggled through my math class, but the parents felt that he was really learning a lot. They were content with C's and D's because they felt it was more important that he be challenged. Not all parents feel that way, but at least I found out at the meeting and we were able to have a good year.

One school in Missouri redefined parent–teacher conferences, dedicating the first conference (held the last week in September) to listening to parents. The director explains,

> We called them "Intake Conferences" and told the participants that we expected the parents to do the talking—and the teachers the listening—75 to 80 percent of the time. "You've known your children for years," I explained in a letter to the parents, "and we've only had them for a few weeks." (Hoerr, 1997, p. 41)

Parents in this school receive a list of questions prior to the conference to consider for discussion. These include questions about the child as well as questions about diversity, such as "Has your child seen family members in situations where they were discriminated against?" and "Have you talked about skin color differences with your child? If so, how did you approach this?" A sample letter to send to parents regarding the intake conference can be found in Resource H.

> Approaching parent–teacher conferences with the attitude that you have specific information to share—and to receive—creates a collegial atmosphere conducive to collaboration.

Approaching parent–teacher conferences with the attitude that you have specific information to share—and to receive—creates a collegial atmosphere conducive to collaboration. Always begin the conference with something positive or humorous about the child. Teacher Kristi Morris, parent of a child with special needs, remembers,

> So many times my husband and I were initially presented with what our son's difficulties were, or how he could improve, or better yet, what we needed to do to make [the teacher's] job easier. We already felt that we were trying our best and this was frustrating.

At the outset of the conference, outline the content of the conference, such as by saying, "I'd like to hear your thoughts about McKenna's reading, and I will share my thoughts as well. We will come up with a game plan today on how we will address her recent reading difficulties." Likewise, at the end of the conference, briefly summarize your discussion, including points made by you and the parent. In addition, delineate responsibilities in your plan of action (Jordan et al., 1998). True collabora- tion means that both you and the parents will be taking action. Even if the bulk of the intervention is for the home, you can offer to facilitate their home activities, such as by sharing resources. It is best to have a written summary sheet that you complete as you close the conference. You can use a generic form for all conferences, such as the one in Resource I.

Pay particular attention to the language you use to discuss sensitive issues with parents. Be aware of the use of educational jargon, particularly regarding disabilities and services, as it may be meaningless or confusing for the parent (Jordan, 1998). Also be tactful when using terms that seem commonplace or innocuous to an educator (e.g., "below average") but may be upsetting to a parent. "Teachers clearly need to reframe in a more positive manner some of the child behaviors they label negatively in order to promote effective collaboration with parents" (Walker-Dalhouse & Dalhouse, 2001, p. 76).

This is particularly true in relation to students from diverse cultures. Realize that what may be viewed as negative behaviors in the classroom may be considered as positive characteristics by the parents. For example, domineering behavior in the classroom may be valued as a leadership quality by the parents, and timidity at school may be a reflection of parents' emphasis on obedience and behavioral inhibition. Parents may also take criticism of the child personally, since parents from some cultural groups bear responsibility for their children's behaviors rather than viewing behavior as resulting from individual characteristics (Okagaki & Diamond, 2000).

Other suggestions for effective parent–teacher conferences include

Always asking parents what kind of person their child is at home and elsewhere

Beginning with two or three positive behaviors and accomplishments before discussing one or two areas where progress is needed

Establishing a time frame for focused work toward remediation (Walker-Dalhouse & Dalhouse, 2001)

In addition, "regardless of a child's performance, it is important to recognize that parents need to first hear what *they* are doing right and what is helping their child" (Walker-Dalhouse & Dalhouse, 2001, p. 79, emphasis added).

Conducting IEP, ITP, and Other Large Group Meetings

Large group meetings, such as Student Study Team, IEP, or ITP meetings, are sometimes necessary but are often difficult to manage interpersonally, since the number of participants impacts group dynamics and communication. Consider the experiences of Tracey Harden, whose 14-year-old daughter has a learning disability and whose 11-year-old son, Ross, has achondroplasia. Ross is in a general education class and receives speech and hearing services, occupational and physical therapy, assistive technology (a laptop computer and amplification device), and sessions with a resource room teacher. In addition, he is assisted by a paraprofessional in the classroom. At a recent conference to discuss changes to Ross's IEP, there were 16 adults—7 from the school, 7 from the Department of Education, Harden, and her lawyer. Harden (2003) recounts the discussion:

> Ross has been struggling academically, and there are different opinions why. According to his teacher and the school principal, it is because of Ross's laziness and bad attitude. According to me and several learning specialists attending the meeting, it is because the demands on his reading and writing have increased, placing extra stress where he is weakest. The school's rigid attitude has not helped things either, in my opinion.
>
> The truth lies somewhere in between. When Ross's teacher describes him as spoiled, I have to suppress a smile, thinking, "prince" would be a more accurate description. As for the "L" word—lazy—I use it at least once a week (sometimes once a day) in reference to Ross. But let the school use it and I go berserk. (p. 25)

When home–school relationships are tense, and sometimes even when they are not, interacting in a large group setting further challenges communication. Typically, the abundance of school personnel creates an intimidating atmosphere. Lytle and Bordin (2001) recommend teachers "make sure that all informal discussion while waiting for the IEP meeting to start is inclusive of everyone present. Avoid discussing items not related to the parents or child. This can make the parent feel like an outsider" (p. 42). Furthermore, it is hard to create an intimate or informal atmosphere with large groups. In a dyad or small group, a difference of opinion can be discussed rationally. In a large group, simple statements turn into declarations made in front of multiple witnesses that must be challenged and defended. Emotions mount, and everything seems more intense when many people are involved. Harden (2003) continues:

> In a large group, simple statements turn into declarations made in front of multiplewitnesses that must be challenged and defended.

> In the meeting this winter at which we discussed his accommodations, things quickly turned ugly. Said the classroom teacher, "I can't believe I am sitting here trying to convince his mother that Ross is capable," to which I responded, "I can't believe you are refusing to make a small accommodation for a child with a disability." In the end, the accommodation was made, and Ross's IEP now calls for extra time for assignments. But it is hard to see this as progress because there is even more ill will on both sides. (p. 26)

Although multiple professionals may need to be present, whenever possible, limit the meeting to a necessary few to avoid overwhelming the parent and creating a combative formal atmosphere.

Reflecting on her reactions, Harden (2003) states,

> There is no question that Ross's attitude (and mine) leave something to be desired at this point. We are both exhausted from dealing with "the school thing," as Ross calls it. . . .

> By now, I know I am part of the problem. Almost anything will set me off, and I am quick to conclude, sometimes wrongly, that schools are biased against Ross because of his handicaps. When I blow up at his teachers, there is always a reason, but my reaction takes on a life of its own because, really, it is about the last 11 years. (p. 26)

Realize that both you and the parent may be reacting to past negative interactions or exhibiting pent-up frustration. In a large group setting, such emotions are difficult to resolve. If blow-ups do occur, try to talk things out with the parent individually.

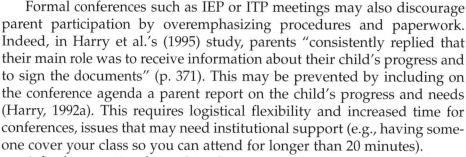

Formal conferences such as IEP or ITP meetings may also discourage parent participation by overemphasizing procedures and paperwork. Indeed, in Harry et al.'s (1995) study, parents "consistently replied that their main role was to receive information about their child's progress and to sign the documents" (p. 371). This may be prevented by including on the conference agenda a parent report on the child's progress and needs (Harry, 1992a). This requires logistical flexibility and increased time for conferences, issues that may need institutional support (e.g., having someone cover your class so you can attend for longer than 20 minutes).

A final suggestion for making large group meetings more welcoming for parents is to consider providing food. Although offering coffee or water is always a nice gesture, providing snacks (or even a meal for lunch-hour meetings) changes the dynamics considerably. A simple bowl of grapes or plate of cookies is a minimal financial investment that can turn a formal meeting into a more informal gathering in which everyone feels more comfortable and cooperative.

Handling Conflicts

As previously discussed, it is imperative to address conflicts as they arise, since even the smallest conflict can escalate and derail a solid working relationship. Acknowledge tension when you sense it, and openly work toward identifying solutions. For example, if you are frustrated that the parents are not following through on their home interventions, discuss whether parents feel they need training, materials, or other supports to get them started. Know when to bring in others to help sort things out. For

instance, if you and a parent cannot agree on how to handle uncompleted homework, enlist another professional who has an understanding of the child's disability and accommodations as well as your teaching demands (e.g., the school psychologist). This individual can serve as an informal mediator or sounding board for you and the parent to help reach an agreement that is satisfactory to both of you. If a parent expresses dissatisfaction about his or her child's lack of progress, invite a speech therapist to demonstrate techniques both you and the parent can use.

Remember that conflict is a naturally occurring phase in your relationships with parents and that it provides opportunity for your relationship to grow. "Few groups are productive immediately; instead, productivity must usually wait until the group matures" (Forsyth, 1990, p. 85). Handling conflicts well takes your collaboration to a more fruitful level.

Dealing With Homework

Homework is necessary for reinforcing skills and concepts you teach, yet it is can also serve an important role in home–school collaboration. Conflicts regarding homework occur frequently, whether it is teachers' frustration over incomplete or missing homework or parents' confusion about assignments. Poor communication between teachers and parents regarding homework is also common, in part because messages and assignments are lost or "intercepted" on the way home (Munk et al., 2001). As students get older, parents report feeling less capable of assisting their children with their homework (Grolnick & Slowiaczek, 1994). A consistent research finding across race and class is that parents desire to help their children but want more guidance from teachers on how to do so (Delgado-Gaitan, 1990; Epstein & Dauber, 1991; Hoover-Dempsey & Sandler, 1995; Hughes, Schumm, & Vaughn, 1999). Thus, there is great potential for teachers to use homework to strengthen home–school connections.

Homework can be specifically designed to inform and involve parents and other family members (Epstein & Van Voorhis, 2001). For example, teachers can create assignments where parents function in the role of a tutor to strengthen students' areas of weakness. Parents can also be encouraged to monitor homework to obtain information that will guide additional interventions, such as changing course schedules (Falbo et al., 2001).

Another approach, however, is to assign "interactive homework," where "parents play supportive roles in discussing homework with their children; they are not asked to teach school skills" (Epstein & Van Voorhis, 2001, p. 186). One example of this is the Teachers Involve Parents in Schoolwork (TIPS) design, in which teachers send home TIPS activities on a regular schedule and allow extra time for their completion (e.g., 2 days) (Epstein & Van Voorhis). Essential elements of this approach are an initial letter to the parent or family member explaining the topic and skill of the assignment, detailed instructions throughout the assignment for students and parents, an invitation for parent comments or questions to the teacher, and parent signature. More information on TIPS can be found in *Teachers Involve Parents in Schoolwork (TIPS) Interactive Homework Training Materials* by Epstein and Van Voorhis (2001). Similarly, Shymansky, Hand, and Yore (2000) describe a science-based project to promote family involvement by using take-home literature-based inquiry, problem-solving, and design activities. Furthermore, assignments that draw upon the family's cultural backgrounds and daily activities can strengthen family–school relationships, such as class lessons and homework based on how mothers use math in sewing (González, Andrade, Civil, & Moll, 2001).

In addition, consider joining with your grade-level colleagues to conduct workshops for parents on how to help their children with homework, such as with reading and writing (Hughes et al., 1999). For example, for parents of younger students, you can conduct a Read-to-Them session in which you demonstrate reading aloud, stopping to elicit the child's comments, and quickly getting back to the story (DeSteno, 2000). Providing parents with specific techniques increases parents' comfort in providing assistance and makes homework assignments more effective.

Sometimes, establishing a classwide organizational system is helpful for minimizing homework hassles such as forgotten books or assignments. This is especially effective at the middle school level where students have multiple subjects and classes but are adjusting to their new level of responsibility. Becky, mother of two teenagers with attention deficit disorder (ADD), shares the organizational system she designed for her daughter that was subsequently adopted by the entire middle school:

> We used lots of color. She picked a color for each subject—Science/green, History/blue, Math/yellow . . . we found folders and spirals to match her color selections and used those colors to label the sections in her daily assignment book. She has homework duo-tangs with one pocket dedicated to "going home" and the other pocket dedicated to "going to school." We also used colored plastic tape to wrap around the spines of the books. This way, when she looked into her locker and knew she had History homework, she knew that she needed all the blue stuff . . . she rarely left something in her locker that she needed at home. (Jaska, 1997)

Some teachers have found that a homework hotline for parents to call to clarify assignments is helpful for reducing confusion. Creating phone trees for parents, particularly bilingual parents, to inform them about specific assignments may also be useful. Other suggestions for minimizing homework conflicts include initialing students' planners daily to ensure accuracy of assignments and using parent–teacher–student meetings to openly address contradictory statements (e.g., "My son says he doesn't have any homework.").

Establishing Boundaries and Other Support Systems

With all of the effort you put into establishing collaborative relationships with parents, you may find yourself in the uncomfortable position of being overused. Deborah Kauffman, an educator with 18 years of teaching experience, recounts her friendship with a particularly needy parent:

> This parent had a reputation for being rather strange in that their appearance was usually harried, ragged dress, unkempt looking. This person was also known as being a trouble maker. . . . Many people within the school system were somewhat intimidated because this mother seemed to have a good grasp of legal issues surrounding public education and meeting the needs of special education students.

> The particular student I had in my classroom was not a special education student, but the siblings were, causing the mom to continually come to me for advice, encouragement and direction. . . . This parent considered me as a friend and more often than not, talk with her would turn to other, more personal matters and

problems that were going on in the home, marriage, and family. I tried to steer conversation away from the intimate details and back into the area of education, but often without much success.

Another teacher friend of mine noticed that I was having difficulty escaping from these conversations and started calling me in my classroom if she saw that this parent was on campus or in my room. The other teacher would tell me that I needed to go to a meeting in the library, staff room, or some other location, to assist me in dismissing the parent after trying to meet her needs, but also cutting the harangue short!

Some parents, like this mother, may cling to you if they find a sympathetic ear and sense a genuine desire to help. You may find yourself overwhelmed with the family's problems and perhaps trapped in a draining relationship. Remember that this type of situation is not beneficial for anyone. Chances are, although you may be the first, you will not be the last person this parent exhausts. Teaching appropriate help-seeking and encouraging respect for boundaries may be difficult, but ultimately provides more assistance than outwardly listening and inwardly wishing for an escape.

First, as Kauffman advises, try not to get emotionally involved. This does not mean being cold and impersonal, but does mean keeping an appropriate professional distance. Since we all have different levels of comfort for helping outside the context of the classroom, use your distress as a guide for where to set the boundaries. For example, if you begin to feel uncomfortable when parents start to talk about marital problems, you may want to say, "Gosh, that sounds really stressful. Do you have a counselor or pastor you can talk to?" You can even use humor to shift the conversation, such as by saying, "I know how to help with long division, but this is beyond me as a teacher!" Reminding parents that you are their child's teacher, not their therapist or social worker, is key.

Next, provide resources and point parents in the right direction. If they are seeking your sympathy for family matters, give them a list of community resources for counseling. Your school counselor, social worker, or psychologist may have already compiled such as listing. Obtain a copy and hand it to the parent when conversations start to become too personal. If they are confused by the special education system, educate them and assist as appropriate, but know when to enlist other professionals (e.g., the special education director, parent liaison, or Student Study Team). Helping parents access and utilize other resources ensures that they will be able to meet their ongoing needs. The Chinese proverb, "If you give a man a fish, you feed him for a day. If you teach a man to fish, you feed him for a lifetime" is applicable in these cases. Although you can provide support and continued encouragement, parents of students with special needs should learn to maximize the resources at their disposal. This means knowing who to turn to for what problem and not overburdening the wrong professional with issues they cannot address.

Last, you may need to overtly discuss limits on your support. For example, one teacher was burdened by a parent who would call or visit the school daily under the pretense of a quick question, but would go on and on about what the child did at home or problems in other classes. This teacher eventually worked out a plan of set times to call or e-mail.

PASSING THE TORCH

The last phase of your working relationship with parents involves ending the relationship well. A natural break occurs when the school year ends, but you can still work to optimize the benefits of your collaboration, not just for yourself, but for your colleagues' advantage as well.

Getting and Giving Feedback

At the end of the year, tell parents what you appreciated about working with them. Chances are no one has ever given them this type of feedback. Although it is always nice to give feedback in person, the end of the school year is a demanding time and your schedule may not allow it. You can use printed cards or certificates; to save time, write them immediately after interacting with the parent (e.g., after a productive conference), but send the note at the end of the year.

In particular, point out strengths parents may have or skills they may have acquired as a result of their determination and hard work. As a teacher, you are in a unique position to offer such positive feedback, and it may make a difference in the parent's life. For example, if you notice that a parent is particularly skilled in organizational or interpersonal skills, you can encourage them to further their talents, such as by seeking community or business partnerships that would benefit the school. Perhaps you discover that one of your parent volunteers is particularly gifted in working with children; you can even encourage the parent to pursue teaching as a career.

Recruiting Parent Mentors

Throughout the year, it is important to encourage parents to build their own support systems. This may be accomplished by pairing families who might complement each other or benefit from friendship. Research has found that parents can be helpful to other parents by imparting practical skills and useful information and providing support for personal growth and for empowerment (Ainbinder et al., 1998). At the end of the year, you may want to enlist select parents who have embraced collaboration to be

Table 8.1 Main Points for Cultivating Collaborative Relationships

In the Beginning

1. Establish credibility as a competent caring educator

2. Be sensitive to parents' cultural views and values

3. Motivate parents to desire collaboration

4. Define specific roles and responsibilities for you and the parent

Maintaining the Relationship

1. Use homework and conferences to deepen your communication and collaboration

2. Be sensitive to parents' feelings and roles in large group meetings

Ending the Relationship

1. Provide parents with positive feedback

2. Encourage parents to use their skills

3. Enlist parents as mentors for other parents

mentors to other parents, particularly parents of your incoming students. This benefits all involved. The mentor parents have an opportunity to share their wisdom about having a child with special needs, about your grade level, and about your teaching style. The incoming parents have another source to seek support from. At the same time, you have an ally—one outside the professional realm—upon whom to call when working with difficult parents. At the end of the school year, thank these particular parents and ask whether they would be willing to help incoming parents. Inform them that you will always contact them first prior to introducing them to other parents, which gives them the opportunity to reconsider their commitment if necessary. Should the occasion arise when you enlist their assistance, be sure to tell the mentors that you do not expect them to defend your actions, but to serve as a support to other parents. At the same time, let the mentee parents know that the mentors are not working under your guidance, but have merely offered to help and share their experiences.

> At the end of the year, you may want to enlist select parents who have embraced collaboration to be mentors to other parents, particularly parents of your incoming students.

PROMOTING A FAMILY-FRIENDLY SCHOOL

As a teacher, your greatest influence is in your classroom, but you also have a role in the school at large. Why is it important to work toward a family-friendly school? Because an overall climate of welcoming parents will make your individual collaborative relationships easier to create and maintain. In addition, if the school as a whole has a family-centered philosophy, administrative policies that allow for flexible scheduling, monetary support, and professional development will facilitate your efforts at collaboration. For example, your administrators may agree to schedule multiple IEP meetings on one day and arrange for a substitute teacher so you will not feel pressured or limited in your participation (Menlove et al., 2001). If your school does not have a plan for increasing parent involvement, you can encourage administrators and other teachers to make the school more family friendly. You may have little control over your administrators, but the squeaky wheel gets the grease, and over time, your ideas may take root.

Schools that are the most successful at partnering with parents have established a give-and-take atmosphere. Parents are expected to be involved, and at the same time, the school is expected to offer real services to the families. Many schools choose to offer classes, such as English as a Second Language or parenting workshops, or to provide information (e.g., monitoring your child's Internet use). Other schools sponsor social events,

where parents and school staff can interact in a nonthreatening environment. For example, one school held Pizza and Puppets Night, where "families paid a nominal fee to eat pizza in the lunchroom with their children and neighbors and enjoy a puppet show" (Hurt, 2000, p. 89). Another school hosted weekly parent breakfasts to get input on a variety of issues (Lewis

& Forman, 2002). Still other schools make their facilities, such as computer classrooms, available for parent use.

Creating a space devoted to families, such as a family learning center, where parents can have coffee while perusing parent education resources or can spend time reading and playing with their children, is particularly

effective in partnering with parents (Hurt, 2000). Some centers allow parents to borrow materials to use with their children at home. This neutral space may also function as a gathering place for parent–teacher conferences or other meetings. Although it is unlikely that you can single-handedly create such a space, by bringing attention to the concept, you may be able to obtain district or PTA funding for the center.

Research has found that the essential element of successful parent involvement programs is having a staff member devoted to parent outreach (Williams & Chavkin, 1989). This individual—a parent coordinator or parent liaison—may be responsible for conducting parent surveys to assess needs and solicit input, for calling parents to invite them to school functions, and for planning periodic family-centered activities (Kirschenbaum, 1999). In addition, the parent coordinator may conduct home visits for hard-to-reach families. The establishment of a parent coordinator, along with other changes, helped School 43, an urban school with 81% of families below the poverty level and 20% from homes where the parents' first language is not English, go from near lowest to the highest levels of parent involvement in its district in just over a year's time (Kirschenbaum). Although social class may impact the *quantity* of time parents can spend at school (e.g., due to work schedules), it does not necessarily influence the *quality* of relationships between parents and teachers (Lewis & Forman, 2002).

Going beyond parent involvement to a truly family-centered school means changing philosophies. Rather than seeing home–school partnerships as a means to an end of educating children, family-centered schools value families more than just the child (McWilliam, Maxwell, & Sloper, 1999). Because schools are often resistant to change (Sarason, 1982), for most schools, this would be a dramatic shift.

BEING REALISTIC

Although most teachers have positive attitudes regarding parent involvement, their classroom practices do not reflect their beliefs (Epstein & Dauber, 1991). Nonetheless, teachers often expect parents to fulfill parent involvement responsibilities, "ranging from teaching their children to behave, to knowing what their children are expected to learn each year, to helping them on those skills" (Epstein & Dauber, p. 304). This double standard is unfortunate, but is probably not consciously held by most teachers. Realistically, however, we cannot expect more from parents than we are willing to do ourselves.

Nevertheless, not all parents will or can respond in kind to your vision of collaboration. They may be hindered by a lack of time, ability, other family pressures, and their own psychological or emotional issues. This does not mean you cannot or should not try to reach the ideal. Because you cannot predict which parent will be your closest partner, it makes sense to attempt collaborating with all parents. One school director stated that "the only way she was able to build relationships with parents was to begin with the assumption that every parent loves his or her child and is doing his or her best" (Lewis & Forman, 2002, p. 84). Remember that

> the parents were the children's first "teachers." They taught their children language (e.g., "doggie," "car"), concepts (e.g., "go bye bye," stove hot), manual skills (e.g., using a spoon . . .), social skills (e.g., "thank you," "I need help"), and even some "academics" like colors, counting, and table games. Depending on the child's disabilities, parents may have varied in their rates of success, but they did teach. (Cutler, 1993, p. 21)

Give parents the benefit of the doubt and assume they have something to offer to you in collaboration. Indeed, the vast majority of parents want to help their children flourish and succeed in school, but need an invitation—and support—from teachers to make it happen.

> Indeed, the vast majority of parents want to help their children flourish and succeed in school, but need an invitation—and support—from teachers to make it happen.

Set a goal to develop strong relationships with a few—maybe three or four—parents this year, and increase the number the following year. But be open to who those parents might be. Just as your most challenging student can become your greatest success story, your most difficult parent may become your greatest ally. Do not be surprised, when you experience a parent's dramatic change from an angry accuser to an indispensable partner, that you find yourself hooked on connecting with parents. Effective home–school collaboration is rewarding—and addicting.

REFLECTING ON YOUR TEACHING

Cultivating solid working relationships with parents of students with special needs requires careful thought and planning. Use the following questions and activities to reflect on your teaching and to facilitate the development of alliances with parents.

1. What is your usual approach to parent–teacher conferences? How much time is devoted to sharing information and how much to listening to parents?

2. How can homework be used in your classroom to improve your relationships with your students' parents and families?

3. How comfortable do you feel interacting with parents on a personal level rather than just as teacher and parent? How does this impact your relationships (e.g., establishing boundaries)?

4. What tangible steps can you take to encourage your school to be more family friendly?

5. Choose a parent of a student with special needs and consider what stage your relationship is in. How can you make the most of that stage to improve your collaboration?

SUMMARY

Building collaborative relationships with parents is a deliberate process. In the beginning, you must establish yourself as a competent caring professional, define the roles you and parents will play, and (sometimes) motivate parents to invest in a working relationship with you. Maintaining collaboration requires good communication, conflict-resolution skills, and sensitivity to relationship boundaries. The final phase of your relationship involves an eye to the future, encouraging continued collaboration with educators, and involving parents with other parents. Throughout the relationship, sensitivity to cultural considerations is paramount. Finally, you can encourage your school to be more family friendly by designating a parent liaison, creating a family center, holding social events for families, and offering classes and other services to parents. Creating an overall school climate that fosters collaborating with parents will facilitate your efforts and benefit all involved, especially the children.

RESOURCE A

Welcome Letter

August 20, 20XX

Dear Parent,

Where did the summer go? In two weeks your child will begin third grade in my classroom. It's going to be an exciting year!

This year, your child will learn basic research skills, develop proficiency in fractions and geometry, be exposed to new technology programs like The Way Things Work CD-ROM, and get dirty in our community garden (great for inspiring poetry). That's just the beginning! We also have several big events planned, including a field trip to the aquarium as part of our Animal Habitats and Adaptations unit and an Ancient Greece and Rome festival.

Please stop by to introduce yourself. I am looking forward to meeting you and your child.

See you in September!

Sincerely,

RESOURCE B

Communication Log

Student's Name:

Parent(s) Name:

Date/Time:	Type of Contact (phone, in-person, letter):	Issues Discussed:	Actions Taken:

RESOURCE C

Letter to Parents of Older Elementary Students

Dear Parents,

Welcome to sixth grade! Your child may be independent and acting old enough to drive, but don't let that fool you. In many ways, you are needed just as much as when your child first started school.

Some parents find it hard to be involved in school as their children get older (sometimes because their kids beg them not to embarrass them!). Please know that I appreciate your involvement and hope to work closely with you to make the most of this important year. I would love to hear your thoughts about your child. Of course, you are always welcome in our classroom, to observe or volunteer, and your participation in special events, like field trips and class projects, is encouraged.

Research shows that children benefit academically by having parents stay involved with their education through high school. One important area is being involved with your child's homework. You can do this by

- Showing your child you value homework as important for increasing learning
- Monitoring the completion of homework
- Assisting your child as needed

Also, keep reading with your child. Read anything that interests you and your child—cookbooks count too!

Check out our class Web site, www.ourclass@school.gov, to see your child's work and get ideas on ways to encourage learning at home, such as through special science projects you can do with the whole family.

I look forward to meeting you. Please let me know what ways I can help you; drop me a note or stop by our classroom. Thank you for your time and efforts!

Sincerely,

RESOURCE D

Letter to Parents of Adolescents

Dear Parent,

Your teenager may not be very talkative about what is going on in school and may even discourage you from coming to school, but don't let that stop you from staying involved in your teen's education.

Research has found that teenagers benefit from parents who are involved in their schooling. Some of the benefits are

♦ Increased student attendance
♦ Better behavior and fewer disciplinary problems
♦ More effort and time spent on homework
♦ Better grades

How can you be involved at the high school level? Some of the most important things you can do are done at home:

1. Talk with your teenager about school.
2. Encourage and praise your teenager's efforts at school.
3. Monitor your teenager's free time and friendships. (Do you know where your teenager is on most afternoons after school?)
4. Offer assistance with homework and projects.
5. Encourage participation in extracurricular activities endorsed by the school, such as sports, music groups, or academic and career clubs.
6. Monitor school progress.

Of course, you can also be involved at school, such as by attending parent meetings and school events or volunteering.

Research also shows that even though teenagers may not say it, they want their parents to be involved (but not embarrass them at school). Let me know how I can help you support your teenager's education.

Sincerely,

RESOURCE E

Parent Observation Sheet

Welcome, Parent! I hope this observation sheet will help you make the most of your visit to our classroom. If you would like, please share your observations with me and with your child at home.

I noticed my child doing these positive things:

1. _____

2. _____

3. _____

When my child interacted with other students . . .

_____

_____

_____

Something my child needs improvement on is . . .

_____

_____

_____

What I can do to help (my child or the class) is . . .

_____

_____

_____

RESOURCE F

Back-to-School Letter

September 5, 20XX

Dear Parent,

Welcome to second grade! I know a lot about teaching second grade, and you know a lot about your child. I hope we can work together to make this year a special one.

Throughout the year, you will receive the "Cheng Chronicles," our classroom newsletter, which will keep you up-to-date about classroom events (like Take Your Parent to School Day), student achievements, and suggestions on how to maximize your child's learning.

That's how you'll hear from me, but I want to hear from you! The easiest ways to reach me are by e-mail (cheng@school.gov) or by dropping a note in my mailbox in the Main Office. Also, please fill out and return the enclosed form so I can get to know you better.

Although the first conference usually is not scheduled until November, you have the option of changing the first conference into an intake conference, scheduled for late September. This conference is different than the typical November conference because it is devoted to *you* teaching me about your child. Please note your preference on the enclosed sheet. (A sign-up sheet for intake conferences will be available at Back-to-School Night, on September 15; November conferences will be scheduled at a later date.)

The classroom door may say "Mrs. Cheng's classroom," but I think of our class as a community. This is your school—come be a part of it. You, the parent, are your child's first, most important, and continuing teacher. I look forward to working together this year for your child's growth.

Sincerely,

Parent name(s): _____

Child's name: _____

Address: _____

Phone numbers: (Home) _____ (Work) _____

E-mail: _____

****

I prefer to help my child by

_____ Volunteering in the classroom

_____ Working one-to-one with a student

_____ Working with a small group of students

_____ Helping with copying, stapling, collating, cutting and pasting materials for class projects

_____ Grading papers

_____ Reading aloud to the class

_____ Making a special presentation on_____

_____ Other_____

_____ Working with my child at home

_____ Checking and helping with homework

_____ Reading at home

_____ Doing special activities that use reading, math, or science

_____ Volunteering at home (for example, preparing materials for special projects)

_____ Chaperoning field trips

_____ Other (for example, providing transportation, calling other parents about events)

Special skills I can offer are (for example, cooking, speaking Spanish):

_____

Additional adult family members (such as grandparents) who would like to be involved:

Name(s): _____ Relationship(s): _____

_____ I would like to have an intake conference in late September. I will attend Back-to-School Night (September 15) to sign up or will contact you to schedule a time if I am unable to attend Back-to-School Night.

_____ I would like to have the traditional parent-teacher conference in November.

Additional comments or information I would like to add:

_____

_____

_____

RESOURCE G

![bar]

Responsibilities of Team Members

The idea behind the team approach is that these individual people sit down together and coordinate their efforts to help the student, regardless of where or how they were trained. For this approach to work, each team member must clearly understand his or her role and responsibilities as a member of the team.

GENERAL EDUCATION CLASSROOM TEACHER

I work with the team to develop and implement appropriate educational experiences for the student during the time that he or she spends in my classroom. I ensure that the student's experiences outside my classroom are consistent with the instruction he or she receives from me. In carrying out my responsibilities, I keep an accurate and continuous record of the student's progress. I am also responsible for referring any other students in my classroom who are at risk and may need specialized services to the school district for an evaluation of their needs.

CONSULTANT OR RESOURCE-ROOM TEACHER

It's my responsibility to coordinate the student's individualized educational plan. I work with each member of the team to assist in selecting, administering, and interpreting appropriate assessment information. I maintain ongoing communication with each team member to ensure that we are all working together to help the student. It is my responsibility to compile, organize, and maintain good, accurate records on each student. I propose instructional alternatives for the student and work with others in the implementation of the recommended instruction. To carry this out, I locate or develop the necessary materials to meet each student's specific needs. I work directly with the student's parents to ensure that they are familiar with what is being taught at school and can reinforce school learning experiences at home.

PARENTS

We work with each team member to ensure that our child is involved in an appropriate educational program. We give information to the team about our child's life outside school and suggest experiences that might be relevant to the home and the community. We also work with our child at home to reinforce what is learned in school. As members of the team, we give our written consent for any evaluations of our child and any changes in our child's educational placement.

SCHOOL PSYCHOLOGIST

I select, administer, and interpret appropriate psychological, educational, and behavioral assessment instruments. I consult directly with team members regarding the student's overall educational development. It is also my responsibility to directly observe the student's performance in the classroom and assist in the design of appropriate behavioral management programs in the school and at home.

SCHOOL ADMINISTRATOR

As the school district's representative, I work with the team to ensure that the resources of my district are used appropriately in providing services to the student. I am ultimately responsible for ensuring that the team's decisions are implemented properly.

These individuals generally constitute the core members of the team, but the team is not limited to this group. Depending on the needs of the student, many other professionals sometimes serve as team members, including speech and language specialists, social workers, school counselors, school nurses, occupational or physical therapists, adaptive physical education teachers, vocational rehabilitation counselors, juvenile court authorities, physicians, and school media coordinators.

RESOURCE H

Intake Conference Letter

Dear _____ ,
        (parent's name)

I am excited to meet you at our intake conference, which is scheduled for

Date: _____

Time: _____

Place: _____

As previously explained, this conference is designed primarily for teachers to listen to parents. Please consider the following questions, which will help me get to know your family and your child. We can discuss some of them at the conference.

How does your child view school?

What are your goals for your child this year?

How do you handle homework (help with it, check it)?

How is your child unique?

What does your child do after school?

How does your family spend time together?

What is your family's heritage?

Does your family have any special cultural or religious traditions?

Also, I am interested in hearing your thoughts about how I can best help your child. Thank you for your time. I look forward to meeting you!

Sincerely,

RESOURCE I

Conference Summary Sheet

Student's Name: _____   Date: _____

Major Points:

1. _____

2. _____

3. _____

Plan of Action:

Teacher responsibilities:

_____

_____

_____

Parent responsibilities:

_____

_____

_____

Plan for Follow-Up:

_____

_____

_____

_____   _____
Teacher signature   Parent signature

RESOURCE J

Additional Resources

The following resources and Web sites may be useful for your information as well as to provide to parents who need additional assistance and support.

General Resources on Special Education

Council for Exceptional Children
1110 N. Glebe Road, Suite 300
Arlington, VA 22201
(703) 620–3660
(703) 264–9446 (TTY)
www.cec.sped.org

The Council for Exceptional Children is an organization for professionals and parents and provides multiple resources, such as training opportunities and legislation updates.

Office of Special Education in the Department of Education
U.S. Department of Education
Office of Special Education
400 Maryland Avenue, SW
Washington, DC 20202
(800) USA-LEARN
(800) 872–5327
www.ed.govabout/offices/list/osers/osep/index.html?src = mr

Numerous publications on special education topics, such as 504 plans and assistive technology, can be obtained from this Web site. Spanish-language versions are available as well.

National Mental Health and Education Center for Children and
Families
National Association of School Psychologists
4340 East West Highway, Suite 402
Bethesda, MD 20874
(301) 657–0270
www.naspweb.org/center/

A public service of the National Association of School Psychologists, this
Web site provides fact sheets for educators and parents on issues such as
discipline and social skills. Appealing sections on mental health issues for
children and teens such as dealing with depression and anxiety can also be
accessed.

Attention Deficit/Hyperactivity Disorder

National Center for Gender Issues and Attention Deficit/
Hyperactivity Disorder
1001 Spring St., Suite 206
Silver Spring, MD 20910
(888) 238–8588
www.addvance.com

This is a not-for-profit organization that promotes awareness, advocacy,
and research on ADHD in women and girls.

Attention Deficit Disorder Association (ADDA)
P.O. Box 543
Pottstown, PA 19464
(484) 945–2101
www.add.org

The ADDA provides information for professionals and parents. Its Web
site has a section specifically for youth, as well as coaching guidelines and
articles on family issues. Of particular interest, a list of accommodations
for 504 plans or the Adaptation and Modifications section of IEPs can be
found at www.add.org/content/ school/list.htm.

Children and Adults with Attention Deficit/Hyperactivity Disorder
(CHADD)
499 N. W. 70th Avenue
Plantation, FL 33317
(305) 587–3700
www.chadd.org

CHADD is a nonprofit organization of 20,000 members and 200 affiliates nationwide that offers support groups, newsletters, and resources.

Learning Disabilities

Learning Disabilities Online
www.ldonline.org

Learning Disabilities Online is a service of The Learning Project at WETA, Washington, D.C., in association with The Coordinated Campaign for Learning Disabilities. It has numerous sections that may be helpful to teachers, as well as a parents' column and a free newsletter.

National Center for Learning Disabilities (NCLD)
381 Park Avenue South, Suite 1401
New York, NY 10016
(888) 575–7373
www.ncld.org

The NCLD Web site offers a section for helping parents advocate for their children, an interactive reading game, and other family resources.

International Dyslexia Association
Chester Building, Suite 380
8600 LaSalle Road
Baltimore, MD 21286
(800) ABCD-123
www.interdys.org

Formerly the Orton Dyslexia Society, the International Dyslexia Association provides information for adults and children with dyslexia.

Other Disabilities

www.heath.gwu.edu

The George Washington University Health Resource Center is responsible for the National Clearinghouse on Postsecondary Education for Individuals with Disabilities. Its Web site has links to topics such as vision impairment, mobility impairment, injury related disabilities, independent living, and more. It also has a resource guide for financial assistance for postsecondary education especially geared toward students with disabilities.

University of Alaska Anchorage
Center for Human Development
2210 Arca Drive
Anchorage, AK 99508
(800) 243–2199
www.alaskachd.org

The Center for Human Development (CHD) is one of 61 University Centers located in every state and territory that attempts to bring together the resources of the university and the community in support of individuals with developmental disabilities. Its Web site provides numerous helpful links related to individuals with disabilities, including several links regarding transition planning.

Other Helpful Information

Information on testing accommodations on the ACT can be obtained via their Web site:

www.act.org/aap/disab/index.html
or by contacting

ACT
500 ACT Drive
Iowa City, IA 52243
(319) 337–1000

Sample Web sites for grandparents raising grandchildren include www.gransplace.com and www.grandparentagain.com, both of which provide information and links to supports.

Selected Texts for Additional Reading

deBettencourt, L. U. (2002). Understanding the differences between IDEA and Section 504. *TEACHING Exceptional Children, 34*(3), 16–23.

This article clearly describes the important ways that IDEA and Section 504 differ and includes a flowchart to determine appropriate services when a student is having difficulty in the classroom.

Epstein, J. L., Sanders, M.G., Simon, B. S., Salinas, K. C., Jansorn, N. R., & Van Voorhis, F. L. (2002). *School, family and community partnerships: Your handbook for action.* Thousand Oaks, CA: Corwin Press.

This research-based book discusses six types of involvement and encourages the development of Action Teams for Partnerships—dynamic groups that plan, implement, evaluate, and continually improve family and community involvement for student success.

Harry, B. (1992). *Cultural diversity, families and the special education system: Communication and empowerment.* New York: Teachers College Press.

Beth Harry has conducted extensive research regarding cultural diversity and families of children with special needs. This is one of her many publications that address the concerns of culturally and linguistically diverse parents.

Novick, B. Z., & Arnold, M. M. (1995). *Why is my child having trouble at school?* New York: Putnam.

Written for parents with numerous case examples, this book discusses core learning disabilities and how to seek professional help.

Parette, P., & McMahan, G. A. (2002). What should we expect of assistive technology? Being sensitive to family goals. *TEACHING Exceptional Children, 35,* 56–61.

This article contains an extensive table that compares family goals and IEP team responses, including potential positive and negative outcomes.

References

Aaroe, L. & Nelson, J. R. (2000). A comparative analysis of teachers', Caucasian parents' and Hispanic parents' views of problematic school survival behaviors. *Education and Treatment of Children, 23,* 314–324.

Abbott, C. F., & Gold, S. (1991). Conferring with parents when you're concerned that their child needs special services. *Young Children, 46*(4), 10–14.

Abrams, E. Z., & Goodman, J. F. (1998). Diagnosing developmental problems in children: Parents and professionals negotiate bad news. *Journal of Pediatric Psychology, 23*(2), 87–98.

Ainbinder, J. G., Blanchard, L. W., Singer, G. H. S., Sullivan, M. E., Powers, L. K., Marquis, J. G., Santelli, B., & Consortium to Evaluate Parent to Parent. (1998). A qualitative study of Parent to Parent support for parents of children with special needs. *Journal of Pediatric Psychology, 23,* 99–109.

Ambady, N., Laplante, D., Nguyen, T., Rosenthal, R., Chaumeton, N., & Levinson, W. (2002). Surgeons' tone of voice: A clue to malpractice history. *Surgery, 132,* 5–9.

American Psychiatric Association. (1994). *Diagnostic and statistical manual of mental disorders* (4th ed.). Washington, DC: Author.

Artiles, A. J., & Trent, S. C. (1994). Overrepresentation of minority students in special education: A continuing debate. *Journal of Special Education, 27,* 410–437.

Bailey, D. B., Skinner, D., Rodriguez, P., Gut, D., & Correa, V. (1999). Awareness, use and satisfaction with services for Latino parents of young children with disabilities. *Exceptional Children, 65,* 367–381.

Baker, M. (2003, March 21). Killing suspect turns himself in. *The Fresno Bee,* pp. B1, 4.

Baranowski, M. D., & Schilmoeller, G. L. (1999). Grandparents in the lives of grandchildren with disabilities: Mothers' perceptions. *Education and Treatment of Children, 22,* 427–446.

Barrett-Kruse, C., Martinez, E., & Carll, N. (1998). Beyond reporting suspected abuse: Positively influencing the development of the student within the classroom. *Professional School Counseling, 1*(3), 57–60.

Barry, E. (1995). Legal issues for prisoners with children. In K. Gabel & D. Johnston (Eds.), *Children of incarcerated parents* (pp. 147–166). New York: Lexington.

Batson, C. D., & Shaw, L. L. (1991). Evidence for altruism: Toward a pluralism of prosocial motives. *Psychological Inquiry, 2,* 107–122.

Bauch, P. A. (2001). School-community partnerships in rural schools: Leadership, renewal, and a sense of place. *Peabody Journal of Education, 76,* 204–221.

Baumeister, R. F., Bushman, B. J., & Campbell, W. K. (2000). Self-esteem, narcissism, and aggression: Does violence result from low self-esteem or from threatened egotism? *Current Directions in Psychological Science, 9,* 26–29.

Bernard, S. (2001). *The mommy and daddy guide to kindergarten: Real-life advice and tips from parents and other experts.* Chicago: Contemporary Books.

Beutler, L. E., Moliero, C., & Talebi, H. (2002). Resistance in psychotherapy: What conclusions are supported by research? *Journal of Clinical Psychology, 58,* 207–217.

Bhat, P., Rapport, M. J. K., & Griffin, C. C. (2000). A legal perspective on the use of specific reading methods for students with learning disabilities. *Learning Disability Quarterly, 23,* 283–297.

Bielick, S., Chandler, K., & Broughman, S. P. (2001). Homeschooling in the United States: 1999. *Education Statistics Quarterly, 3*(3), 25–32.

Boutte, G. S., Keepler, D. L., Tyler, V. S., & Terry, B. Z. (1992). Effective techniques for involving "difficult" parents. *Young Children, 47*(3), 19–22.

Brady, B. A., Tucker, C. M., Harris, Y. R., & Tribble, I. (1992). Association of academic achievement with behavior among Black students and White students. *Journal of Educational Research, 86,* 43–51.

Bryan, T., Mathur, S., & Sullivan, K. (1996). The impact of positive mood on learning. *Learning Disability Quarterly, 19,* 153–162.

Campbell, S. B., Simon, R., Weithorn, L., Krikston, D., & Connolly, K. (1980). Successful foster homes need parent-child match. *Journal of Social Welfare, 6,* 47–60.

Caplan, G., & Caplan, R. B. (1993). *Mental health consultation and collaboration.* San Francisco: Jossey-Bass.

Carnine, D., & Granzin, A. (2001). Setting learning expectations for students with disabilities. *School Psychology Review, 30,* 466–472.

Chavira, V., Lopez, S. R., Blacher, J., & Shapiro, J. (2000). Latina mothers' attributions, emotions and reactions to the problem behaviors of their children with developmental disabilities. *Journal of Child Psychology and Psychiatry, 41,* 245–252.

Chrispeels, J. H., & Rivero, E. (2001). Engaging Latino families for student success: How parent education can reshape parents' sense of place in the education of their children. *Peabody Journal of Education, 76,* 119–169.

Cohen, R. (2002, November 30). Pick your battles with the teacher. *The Fresno Bee,* p. F1.

Collet-Klingenberg, L. L. (1998). The reality of best practices in transition: A case study. *Exceptional Children, 65,* 67–79.

Coots, J. J. (1998). Family resources and parent participation in schooling activities for their children with developmental delays. *Journal of Special Education, 31,* 498–520.

Council for Exceptional Children. (1994). Statistical profile of special education in the United States, 1994. *Supplement to TEACHING Exceptional Children, 26*(3), 1–4.

Cox, C. B. (2000). Why grandchildren are going to and staying at grandmother's house and what happens when they get there. In C. B. Cox (Ed.), *To grandmother's house we go and stay* (pp. 3–19). New York: Springer.

Cox, C. B. (2002). Empowering African American custodial grandparents. *Social Work, 47,* 45–54.

Cutler, B. C. (1993). *You, your child, and special education: A guide to making the system work.* Baltimore: Paul H. Brookes.

Danesco, E. R. (1997). Parental beliefs on childhood disability: Insights on culture, child development and intervention. *International Journal of Disability, Development and Education, 44,* 41–51.

Davies, D. (1993). Benefits and barriers to parent involvement: From Portugal to Boston to Liverpool. In N. Chavkin (Ed.), *Families and schools in a pluralistic society* (pp. 205–216). Albany: State University of New York Press.

deBettencourt, L. U. (2002). Understanding the differences between IDEA and Section 504. *TEACHING Exceptional Children, 34*(3), 16–23.

Delgado-Gaitan, C. (1990). *Literacy for empowerment: The role of parents in children's education.* New York: Falmer Press.

Dell, D. L. (2003, February 9). A gentleman, a revolutionary: Remembering Arthur Ashe, as if he could ever be forgotten. *The New York Times,* Section 8, p. 7.

Delpit, L. D. (1995). *Other people's children: Cultural conflict in the classroom.* New York: New Press.

Denby, R., Rindfleisch, N., & Bean, G. (1999). Predictions of foster parents' satisfaction and intent to continue to foster. *Child Abuse and Neglect, 23,* 287–303.

Derby, K. M., Wacker, D. P., Berg, W., DeRaad, A., Ulrich, S., Asmus, J., Harding, J., Prouty, A., Laffey, P., & Stoner, E. A. (1997). The long-term effects of functional communication training in home setting. *Journal of Applied Behavior Analysis, 30,* 507–531.

Deslandes, R., & Cloutier, R. (2002). Adolescents' perception of parental involvement in schooling. *School Psychology International, 23,* 220–232.

Deslandes, R., Royer, E., Potvin, P., & LeClerc, D. (1999). Patterns of home and school partnership for general and special education students at the secondary level. *Exceptional Children, 65,* 496–506.

DeSteno, N. (2000). Parent involvement in the classroom: The fine line. *Young Children, 55*(3), 13–17.

DeToledo, S., & Brown, D. (1995). *Grandparents as parents: A survival guide for raising a second family.* New York: Guilford.

Detterman, D. K., & Thompson, L. A. (1997). What is so special about special education? *American Psychologist, 52,* 1082–1090.

Dinnebeil, L. A., Hale, L. M., & Rule, S. (1996). A qualitative analysis of parents' and service coordinators' descriptions of variables that influence collaborative relationships. *Topics in Early Childhood Special Education, 16,* 322–347.

Dinnebeil, L. A., Hale, L. M., & Rule, S. (1999). Early intervention program practices that support collaboration. *Topics in Early Childhood Special Education, 19,* 225–235.

Dodd, A. W. (1998). What can educators learn from parents who oppose curricular and classroom practices? *Journal of Curriculum Studies, 30,* 461–477.

Dodd, A. W. (1992). *A parent's guide to innovative education: Working with teachers, schools and your children for real learning.* Chicago: Noble Press.

Dowdell, E. B. (1995). Caregiver burden: Grandmothers raising their high risk grandchildren. *Journal of Psychosocial Nursing, 33,* 27–30.

Downing, J., & Downing, S. (1991). Consultation with resistant parents. *Elementary School Guidance and Counseling, 25,* 296–301.

Dunklee, O. R., & Shoop, R. J. (2001). *The principal's quick reference guide to school law: Reducing liability, litigation and other potential legal tangles.* Thousand Oaks, CA: Corwin Press.

Edwards, A., & Warin, J. (1999). Parental involvement in raising the achievement of primary school pupils: Why bother? *Oxford Review of Education, 25,* 325–341.

Enright, R. (2001). *Forgiveness is a choice.* Washington, DC: American Psychological Association.

Epstein, J. L. (1985). Home-school connections in schools of the future: Implications of research on parent involvement. *Peabody Journal of Education, 62*(2), 18–41.

Epstein, J. L. (1986). Parents' reactions to teacher practices of parent involvement. *Elementary School Journal, 86,* 277–294.

Epstein, J. L. (1991). Effects on student achievement of teachers' practices of parent involvement. *Advances in Reading/Language Research, 5,* 261–276.

Epstein, J. L. (1995). School/family/community partnerships: Caring for the child we share. *Phi Delta Kappan, 76,* 701–712.

Epstein, J. L. (2000). *School and family partnerships: Preparing educators and improving schools.* Boulder, CO: Westview.

Epstein, J. L., & Connors, L. J. (1995). School and family partnerships in the middle grades. In B. Rutherford (Ed.), *Creating family/school partnerships* (pp. 137–166). Columbus, OH: National Middle School Association.

Epstein, J. L., & Dauber, S. L. (1991). School programs and teacher practices of parent involvement in inner-city elementary and middle schools. *Elementary School Journal, 91*(3), 289–305.

Epstein, J. L., & Van Voorhis, F. L. (2001). *Teachers Involve Parents in Schoolwork (TIPS) interactive homework training materials.* Baltimore, MD: Johns Hopkins University, Center on School, Family, and Community Partnerships.

Epstein, J. L., & Van Voorhis, F. L. (2001). More than minutes: Teachers' roles in designing homework. *Educational Psychologist, 36,* 181–193.

Falbo, T., Lein, L., & Amador, N. A. (2001). Parental involvement during the transition to high school. *Journal of Adolescent Research, 16,* 511–529.

Fielding, P. S. (1990). Mediation in special education. *Reading, Writing and Learning Disabilities, 6,* 41–52.

Fisher, R., Ury, W., & Patton, B. (1991). *Getting to yes: Negotiating agreement without giving in.* New York: Penguin Books.

Fitzgerald, L. M., & Göncü, A. (1993). Parent involvement in urban early childhood education: A Vygotskian approach. In S. Reifel (Ed.), *Advances in early childhood education and day care: Perspectives on developmentally appropriate practice* (pp. 27–35). Greenwich, CT: JAI Press.

Flett, A., & Conderman, G. (2001). Enhance the involvement of parents from culturally and linguistically diverse backgrounds. *Intervention in School and Clinic, 37,* 53–55.

Florence County School District Four v. Carter, (91–1523), 510 U.S. 7 (1993).

Ford, M. S., Follmer, R., & Litz, K. K. (1998). School-family partnerships: Parents, children, and teachers benefit! *Teaching Children Mathematics, 4*(6), 310–312.

Forgas, J. P. (2002). Feeling and doing: Affective influences on interpersonal behavior. *Psychologial Inquiry, 13,* 1–28.

Forsyth, D. R. (1990). *Group dynamics* (2nd ed.). Pacific Grove, CA: Brooks/Cole.

Friedman, B. B. (1998). What early childhood educators need to know about divorced fathers. *Early Childhood Education Journal, 25,* 239–241.

Friedman, B. B., & Berkeley, T. R. (2002). Encouraging fathers to participate in the school experiences of young children: The teacher's role. *Early Childhood Education Journal, 29,* 209–213.

Garlington, J. A. (1991). *Helping dreams survive: The story of a project involving African-American families in the education of their children.* Washington, DC: National Committee for Citizens in Education.

Gaudin, J. M., & Sutphen, R. (1993). Foster care vs. extended family care for children of incarcerated mothers. *Journal of Offender Rehabilitation, 19*(3/4), 129–147.

Geenen, S., Powers, L. E., & Lopez-Vasquez, A. (2001). Multicultural aspects of parent involvement in transition planning. *Exceptional Children, 67,* 265–282.

Glass, J. C., Jr. & Huneycutt, T. L. (2002). Grandparents parenting grandchildren: Extent of situation, issues involved and educational implications. *Educational Gerontology, 28,* 139–161.

Gollnick, D. M., & Chinn, P. C. (1994). *Multicultural education in a pluralistic society* (4th ed.). New York: Merrill.

González, N., Andrade, R., Civil, M., & Moll, L. (2001). Bridging funds of distributed knowledge: Creating zones of practice in mathematics. *Journal of Education of Students Placed at Risk, 6,* 115–132.

Gorman, J. C. (1998). Parenting attitudes and practices of immigrant Chinese mothers of adolescents. *Family Relations, 47,* 73–80.

Green, S. E. (2001). Grandma's hands: Parental perceptions of the importance of grandparents as secondary caregivers in families of children with disabilities. *International Journal of Aging and Human Development, 53,* 11–33.

Greene, J. (1998). *How teachers can avoid being sued: Law and American education.* (Report No. SP 038968). (ERIC Document Reproduction Service No. ED437381)

Grolnick, W. S., & Slowiaczek, M. L. (1994). Parents' involvement in children's schooling: A multidimensional conceptualization and motivational model. *Child Development, 65,* 237–252.

Gross, J. (2003, April 13). Nudging toward normal. *New York Times,* Education Life, Section 4A, pp. 27–28, 32, 33.

Hancock, R. (1998). Building home-school liaison into classroom practice: A need to understand the nature of a teacher's working day. *British Educational Research Journal, 24,* 399–414.

Harden, G. D. (1993). Parents say the darndest things. *Principal, 72*(3), 40–41.

Harden, T. (2003, April 13). Raising Ross. *New York Times,* Section 4A, p. 24–26.

Harry, B. (1992a). An ethnographic study of cross-cultural communication with Puerto Rican American families in the special education system. *American Educational Research Journal, 29,* 471–494.

Harry, B. (1992b). *Cultural diversity, families and the special education system: Communication and empowerment.* New York: Teachers' College Press.

Harry, B. (1998). Parental visions of "una vida normal/a normal life": Cultural variations on a theme. In L. H. Meyer, H.-S. Park, M. Grenot-Scheyer, I. S. Schwartz, & B. Harry (Eds.), *Making friends: The influences of culture and development* (pp. 47–62). Baltimore: Paul H. Brookes.

Harry, B. (2002). Trends and issues in serving culturally diverse families of children with disabilities. *Journal of Special Education, 36*(3), 131–147.

Harry, B., Allen, N., & McLaughlin, M. (1995). Communication versus compliance: African American parents' involvement in special education. *Exceptional Children, 61*, 364–377.

Harry, B., & Anderson, M. G. (1994). The disproportionate placement of African-American males in special education programs: A critique of the process. *Journal of Negro Education, 63*, 602–619.

Harry, B., Kalyanpur, M., & Day, M. (1999). *Building cultural reciprocity with families.* Baltimore: Paul H. Brookes.

Harry, B., Rueda, R., & Kalyanpur, M. (1999). Cultural reciprocity in sociocultural perspective: Adapting the normalization principle for family collaboration. *Exceptional Children, 66*, 123–136.

Hartwig, L. J. (1984). Living with dyslexia: One parent's experience. *Annals of Dyslexia, 34*, 313–318.

Hastings, R. P. (1997). Grandparents of children with disabilities: A review. *International Journal of Disability, Development and Education, 44*, 329–340.

Hayes, K. G. (1992). Attitudes toward education: Voluntary and involuntary immigrants from the same families. *Anthropology & Educational Quarterly, 23*, 250–267.

Henderson, A. T., & Berla, N. (1996). *A new generation of evidence: The family is critical to student achievement.* Washington, DC: Center for Law and Education.

Hewison, J. (1988). The long-term effectiveness of parental involvement in reading: A follow-up to the Haringey reading project. *British Journal of Educational Psychology, 58*, 184–190.

Hickson, G. B., Clayton, E. W., Entman, S. S., Miller, C. S., Githens, P. B., Whetten-Goldstein, K., & Sloan, F. A. (1994). Obstetricians' prior malpractice experience and patients' satisfaction with care. *Journal of the American Medical Association, 272,*1583–1587.

Hickson, G. B, Federspiel, C. F., Pichert, J. W., Miller, C. S., Gauld-Jaeger, J., & Bost, P. (2002a) Patient complaints and malpractice risk. *Journal of the American Medical Association, 287*, 2951–2957.

Hickson, G. B., Pichert, J., Miller, C. S., Gauld-Jaeger, J., Federspiel, C. F., & Bost, P. (2002b). Discussion. *Journal of the American Medical Association, 288*, 1586.

Hill, R. (1993). *Research on the African American family: A holistic perspective.* Boston: University of Massachusetts.

Hoerr, T. R. (1997). When teachers listen to parents. *Principal, 77*(2), 40–42.

Hogan, J. (1990). Advocating for children: A parents' guide. *Reading, Writing, and Learning Disabilities, 6*, 81–88.

Hoover-Dempsey, K., & Sandler, H. (1995). Parent involvement in children's education: Why does it make a difference? *Teachers College Record, 97*(2), 310–331.

Hughes, M. T., Schumm, J. S., & Vaughn, S. (1999). Home literacy activities: Perceptions and practices of Hispanic parents of children with learning disabilities. *Learning Disability Quarterly, 22*, 224–235.

Hunt, H., & West, S. (1997). Training requirements for foster parents. *Fostering Perspectives* [Online], 1(1), Retrieved from www.ssw.unc.edu/fcrp

Hurt, J. A. (2000). Create a parent place: Make the invitation for family involvement real. *Young Children, 55*(5), 88–92.

Hutchins, M. & Renzaglia, A. (1998). Interviewing families for effective transition to employment. *TEACHING Exceptional Children, 30*, 66–69.

Ickes, W. (Ed.) (1997). *Empathic accuracy.* New York: Guilford Press.

Individuals with Disabilities Education Act (IDEA) Amendments of 1997, 20 U.S.C., § 1400–1485.8 (1997). (ERIC Document Reproduction Service No. ED419322)

Jacob, J. (2002, October 21). You're ready for the exam, but where's the patient? *American Medical News,* pp. 19, 21.

Jacob, S., & Hartshorne, T. (1991). *Ethics and law for school psychologists.* Brandon, VT: Clinical Psychology.

Jaska, P. (1997, June). Focus on ADD/ADHD. *Online Psychology Forum* [Online]. Retrieved from www.add.org/content/interview/becky/htm.

Johnson, D. R., Stodden, R. A., Emanuel, E. J., Luecking, R., & Mack, M. (2002). Current challenges facing secondary education and transition services: What research tells us. *Exceptional Children, 68,* 519–532.

Jones, R. (2001). How parents can support learning. *American School Board Journal, 188*(9), 18–22.

Jordan, L., Reyes-Blanes, M. E., Peel, B. B., Peel, H. A., & Lane, H. B. (1998). Developing teacher-parent partnerships across cultures: Effective parent conferences. *Intervention in School and Clinic, 33*(3), 141–147.

Kalyanpur, M. & Harry, B. (1997). A posture of reciprocity: A practical approach to collaboration between professionals and parents of culturally diverse backgrounds. *Journal of Child and Family Studies, 6,* 487–509.

Kalyanpur, M., Harry, B., & Skrtic, T. (2000). Equity and advocacy expectations of culturally diverse families' participation in special education. *International Journal of Disability, Development and Education, 47,* 119–136.

Kalyanpur, M., & Rao, S. (1991). Empowering low-income black families of handicapped children. *American Journal of Orthopsychiatry, 61,* 523–532.

Kaufman, H. O. (2001). Skills for working with all families. *Young Children, 56*(4), 81–83.

Kerem, E., Fishman, N., & Josselson, R. (2001). The experience of empathy in everyday relationships: Cognitive and affective elements. *Journal of Social and Personal Relationships, 18,* 709–729.

Kirschenbaum, H. (1999). Night and day: Succeeding with parents at School 43. *Principal, 78*(3), 20–23.

Kosmoski, G. J., & Pollack, D. R. (2001). *Managing conversations with hostile adults.* Thousand Oaks, CA: Corwin Press.

Kübler-Ross, E. (1969). *On Death and Dying.* New York: Macmillan.

Lake, J. F., & Billingsley, B. S. (2000). An analysis of factors that contribute to parent-school conflict in special education. *Remedial and Special Education, 21,* 240–251.

LaMorte, M. W. (1996). *School law: Cases and concepts.* Boston: Allyn & Bacon.

Lardieri, L. A., Blacher, J., & Swanson, H. L. (2000). Sibling relationships and parent stress in families of children with and without learning disabilities. *Learning Disability Quarterly, 23,* 105–116.

Lee, S. (1994). *Family-school connections and students' education: Continuity and change of family involvement from the middle grades to high school.* Unpublished doctoral dissertation, Johns Hopkins University, Baltimore, MD.

Leon, E. (1996). *Challenges and solutions for educating migrant students.* Lansing, MI: Department of Education. (ERIC Document Reproduction Service No. ED393615)

Lerner, J. (1993). *Learning disabilities: Theories, diagnosis and teaching Strategies* (6th ed.). Boston: Houghton Mifflin.

Levinson, W., Roter, D. L., Mullooly, J. P., Dull, V. T., & Frankel, R. M. (1997). Physician-patient communication: The relationship with malpractice claims among primary care physicians and surgeons. *Journal of the American Medical Association, 277*, 553–559.

Lewis, A. E., & Forman, T. A. (2002). Contestation or collaboration? A comparative study of home-school relations. *Anthropology & Education Quarterly, 33*, 60–89.

Leyser, Y., & Dekel, G. (1991). Perceived stress and adjustment in religious Jewish families with a child who is disabled. *Journal of Psychology, 125*, 427–438.

Lopez, N. (2002). Race-gender experiences and schooling: Second generation Dominican, West Indian, and Haitian youth in New York City. *Race Ethnicity and Education, 5*, 67–89.

Luskin, F. (2002). *Forgive for good: A proven prescription for health and happiness.* New York: HarperCollins.

Lytle, R. K., & Bordin, J. (2001). Enhancing the IEP team: Strategies for parents and professionals. *TEACHING Exceptional Children, 33*(5), 40–44.

Maiers, A. & Nistler, R. J. (1998). Changing parent roles in school: Effects of a school-based family literacy program in an urban first-grade classroom. *National Reading Conference Yearbook, 47*, 221–231.

Mandal, M., Bryden, M. P., & Bulman-Fleming, M. B. (1996). Similarities and variations in facial expressions of emotions: Cross-cultural evidence. *International Journal of Psychology, 31*, 49–58.

Manning, D., & Schindler, P. J. (1997). Communicating with parents when their children have difficulties. *Young Children, 52*(5), 27–33.

Martin, R., Watson, D., & Wan, C. K. (2000). A three-factor model of trait anger: Dimensions of affect, behavior and cognition. *Journal of Personality, 68*, 869–897.

Matier, P., & Ross, A. (2003, March 3). Oakland's schools fiscal feud fueled by politics of power. *San Francisco Chronicle*, Section B, p. 1, 2.

Matlosz, F. C. (2002, August 24). Hmong threaten class ban. *The Fresno Bee*, p. A1.

Matsumoto, D. (1993). Ethnic differences in affect intensity, emotion judgments, display rule attitudes, and self-reported emotional expression in an American sample. *Motivation and Emotion, 17*, 107–123.

May, M. (2003, March 5). Oakland school board Oks $17 million in budget cuts. *San Francisco Chronicle*, Section A, p. 19.

McCullough, M. E. (2001). Forgiveness: Who does it and how do they do it? *Current Directions in Psychological Science, 10*(6), 194–197.

McCullough, M. E., Bellah, C. G., Kilpatrick, S. D., & Johnson, J. L. (2001). Vengefulness: Relationships with forgiveness, rumination, well-being and the Big Five. *Personality and Social Psychology Bulletin, 27*, 601–610.

McCullough, M. E., & Worthington, E. L. Jr. (1999). Religion and the forgiving personality. *Journal of Personality, 67*, 1141–1164.

McDowell, S. A., Sanchez, A.R., & Jones, S. S. (2000). Participation and perception: Looking at homeschooling though a multicultural lens. *Peabody Journal of Education, 75*, 124–146.

McEwan, E. K. (1998). *How to deal with parents who are angry, troubled, afraid or just plain crazy.* Thousand Oaks, CA: Corwin Press.

McLain, P. (2002, September 29). Hand-me-downs. *New York Times Magazine*, p. 124.

McNair, J., & Rusch, E. R. (1991). Parent involvement in transition programs. *Mental Retardation, 29*(2), 93–101.

McNeal, R. B. (1999). Parental involvement as social capital: Differential effectiveness on science achievement, truancy and dropping out. *Social Forces, 78,* 117–144.

McWilliam, R. A., Maxwell, K. L., & Sloper, K. M. (1999). Beyond "involvement": Are elementary schools ready to be family-centered? *School Psychology Review, 28,* 378–394.

Menlove, R. R., Hudson, P. J., & Suter, D. (2001). A field of dreams: Increasing general education teacher participation in the IEP development process. *TEACHING Exceptional Children, 33*(5), 28–33.

Merriam-Webster's Collegiate Dictionary (11th ed.). (2003). Springfield, MA: Merriam-Webster.

Modell, S. J., & Valdez, L. (2002). Beyond bowling: Transition planning for students with disabilities. *TEACHING Exceptional Children, 34*(6), 46–53.

Morningstar, M. E., Turnbull, A. P., & Turnbull, H. R. (1995). What do students with disabilities tell us about the importance of family involvement in the transition from school to adult life? *Exceptional Children, 62*(3), 249–261.

Mosley-Howard, G. S., & Evans, C. B. (2000). Relationships and contemporary experiences of the African American family: An ethnographic case study. *Journal of Black Studies, 30,* 428–452.

Muller, C. (1993). Parent involvement and academic achievement. In B. S. & J. S. Coleman (Eds.), *Parents, Their Children, and Schools* (pp.77–113). Boulder, CO: Westview.

Munk, D. D., Bursuck, W. D., Epstein, M. H., Jayanthi, M., Nelson, J., & Polloway, E. A. (2001). Homework communication problems: Perspectives of special and general education parents. *Reading & Writing Quarterly, 17,* 189–203.

National Clearinghouse for Professions in Special Education. (1991). *The severe shortage of minority personnel.* Washington, DC: U.S. Department of Education, National Center for Education Statistics.

Neuberg, S. L., Cialdini, R. B., Brown, S.I., Luce, C., Sagarin, B. J., & Lewis, B. (1997). Does empathy lead to anything more than superficial helping? Comment on Batson et al. (1997). *Journal of Personality and Social Psychology, 73,* 510–516.

Nowicki, S., Jr., Glanville, D., & Demertzis, A. (1998). A test of the ability to recognize emotion in the facial expressions of African American adults. *Journal of Black Psychology, 24,* 335–350.

Nunnelley, J. C., & Fields, T. (1999). Anger, dismay, guilt, anxiety—The realities and roles in reporting child abuse. *Young Children, 54*(5), 74–79.

Okagaki, L., & Diamond, K. E. (2000). Responding to cultural and linguistic differences in the beliefs and practices of families with young children. *Young Children, 55*(3), 74–80.

Okun, B. F. (1992). *Effective helping: Interviewing and counseling techniques* (4th ed.). Pacific Grove, CA: Brooks/Cole.

Orme, J. G., & Buehler, C. (2001). Foster family characteristics and behavioral and emotional problems of foster children: A narrative review. *Family Relations, 50,* 3–15.

Parette, P., & McMahan, G. A. (2002). What should we expect of assistive technology? Being sensitive to family goals. *TEACHING Exceptional Children, 35,* 56–61.

Patton, J. M. (1998). The disproportionate representation of African Americans in special education: Looking behind the curtain for understanding and solutions. *Journal of Special Education, 32*, 25–31.

Peck Peterson, S. M., Derby, K. M., Berg, W. K., & Horner, R. H. (2002). Collaboration with families in the functional behavior assessment of and intervention for severe behavior problems. *Education and Treatment of Children, 25*, 5–26.

Quiroz, B., Greenfield, P. M., & Altchech, M. (1999). Bridging cultures with a parent-teacher conference. *Educational Leadership, 56*(7), 68–70.

Rao, S. S. (2000). Perspectives of an African American mother on parent-professional relationships in special education. *Mental Retardation, 38*, 475–488.

Ramirez, F. (2001). Technology and parental involvement. *The Clearing House, 75*, 30–31.

Ribas, W. B. (1998). Tips for reaching parents. *Educational Leadership, 56*, 83–85.

Rodriguez Mosquera, P. M., Manstead, A. S. R., & Fischer, A. H. (2002). The role of honour concerns in emotional reactions to offences. *Cognition and Emotion, 16*, 143–163.

Rothenberg, D. (1996). *Grandparents as parents: A primer.* Urbana, IL: ERIC Clearinghouse on Elementary and Early Childhood Education. (ERIC Document Reproduction Service No. ED401044)

Sarason, S. B. (1982). *The culture of the school and the problem of change* (2nd ed.). Boston: Allyn & Bacon.

Schloss, P. J., Alper, S., & Jayne, D. (1994). Self-determination for persons with disabilities: Choice, risk and dignity. *Exceptional Children, 60*, 215–255.

Schneider, B., & Lee, Y. (1990). A model for academic success: The school and home environment of East Asian students. *Anthropology and Education Quarterly, 21*, 358–377.

Schneider, M., Marschall, M., Teske, P., & Roch, C. (1998). School choice and culture wars in the classroom: What different parents seek from education. *Social Science Quarterly, 79*, 498–501.

Scorgie, K., Wilgosh, L., & McDonald, L. (1996). A qualitative study of managing life when a child has a disability. *Developmental Disabilities Bulletin, 24*(2), 68–90.

Seligman, M., & Darling, R. B. (1989). *Ordinary families, special children: A systems approach to childhood disability.* New York: Guilford Press.

Seligman, M., & Darling, R. B. (1997). *Ordinary families, special children: A systems approach to childhood disability* (2nd ed.). New York: Guilford Press.

Serpell, R. (1994). Negotiating a fusion of horizons: A process view of cultural validation in developmental psychology. *Mind, Culture, and Activity, 1*, 43–68.

Sheridan, S. M., & Kratochwill, T. R. (1992). Behavioral parent-teacher consultation: Conceptual and research considerations. *Journal of School Psychology, 30*, 117–139.

Sherif, M., Harvey, O. J., White, B. J., Hood, W. R., & Sherif, C. W. (1961). *Intergroup conflict and cooperation: The robbers cave experiment.* Norman, OK: Institute of Group Relations.

Shymansky, J. A., Hand, B. M., & Yore, L. D. (2000). Empowering families in hands-on science programs. *School Science and Mathematics, 100*, 48–61.

Simms, M. D., & Horwitz, S. M. (1996). Foster home environments: A preliminary report. *Developmental and Behavioral Pediatrics, 17*, 170–175.

Singh, K., Bickley, P. G., Keith, T. Z., Keith, P. B., Trivette, P., & Anderson, E. (1995). The effects of four components of parental involvement on eighth-grade student achievement: Structural analysis of NELS-88 data. *School Psychology Review, 24,* 299–317.

Siu, S-F. (1994). Taking no chances: A profile of a Chinese-American family's support for school success. *Equity and Choice, 10*(2), 23–32.

Smith, T. E. C. (1981). Status of due process hearings. *Exceptional Children, 48,* 232–236.

Smith, A. B., Dannison, L. L., & Vach-Hasse, T. (1998). When "Grandma" is "Mom." *Childhood Education, 75,* 12–16.

Spindler, G., & Spindler, L. (1994). What is cultural therapy? In G. Spindler & L. Spindler (Eds.), *Pathways to cultural awareness: Cultural therapy with teachers and students* (pp. 1–33). Thousand Oaks, CA: Corwin Press.

Steere, D. E., & Cavaiuolo, D. (2002). Connecting outcomes, goals, and objectives in transition planning. *TEACHING Exceptional Children, 34*(6), 54–59.

Steinberg, L, Lamborn, S. D., Dornbusch, S. M., & Darling, N. (1992). Impact of parenting practices on adolescent achievement: Authoritative parenting, school involvement, and encouragement to succeed. *Child Development, 63,* 1266–1281.

Stowitschek, J. J., Lovitt, T. C., & Rodriguez, J. A. (2001). Patterns of collaboration in secondary education for youth with special needs: Profiles of three high schools. *Urban Education, 36,* 93–128.

Stucke, T. S., & Sporer, S. L. (2002). When a grandiose self-image is threatened: Narcissism and self-concept clarity as predictors of negative emotions and aggression following ego-threat. *Journal of Personality, 70,* 509–532.

Summers, J. A., Dell'Oliver, C., Turnbull, A. P., Benson, H. A., Santelli, B., Campbell, M., & Siegel-Causey, E. (1990). Examining the individualized family service plan process: What are family and practitioner preferences? *Topics in Early Childhood Special Education, 10,* 78–99.

Swick, K. J. (1999). Empowering homeless and transient children/families: An ecological framework for early childhood teachers. *Early Childhood Education Journal, 26,* 195–201.

Talbert-Johnson, C. (1998). Why so many African-American children in special ed? *School Business Affairs, 64*(4), 30–35.

Tao, L., & Boulware, B. (2002). E-mail: Instructional potentials and learning opportunities. *Reading and Writing Quarterly, 18,* 285–288.

Taylor, S. E., Peplau, L. A., & Sears, D. O. (1997). *Social psychology* (9th ed.). Upper Saddle River, NJ: Prentice Hall.

Törestad, B. (1990). What is anger provoking? A psychophysical study of perceived causes of anger. *Aggressive Behavior, 16,* 9–26.

Trainor, A. (2002). Self-determination for students with learning disabilities: Is it a universal value? *Qualitative Studies in Education, 15,* 711–725.

Trueba, H., & Delgado-Gaitan, C. (Eds.) (1988). *School and society: Learning content through culture.* New York: Praeger.

Trusty, J. (1996). Relationship of parent involvement in teens' career development to teens' attitudes, perceptions and behavior. *Journal of Research and Development in Education, 30,* 317–323.

Tuckman, B. W. (1965). Developmental sequences in small groups. *Psychological Bulletin, 63,* 384–399.

Tuckman, B. W., & Jensen, M. A. (1977). Stages of small group development revisited. *Group and Organizational Studies, 2,* 419–427.

Turnbull, H. R., & Turnbull, A. P. (1998). *Free appropriate public education: The law and children with disabilities* (5th ed.). Denver, CO: Love.

Ury, W. (1991). *Getting past no: Negotiating with difficult people.* New York: Bantam Books.

U.S. Census Bureau. (1990, March). *Census of Population and Housing Summary* (Current population reports). Washington, DC: Author.

U.S. General Accounting Office. (1989). *Special education: The Attorney Fees Provision of Public Law 99-372.* Washington, DC: U.S. Government Printing Office.

Vadasy, P. F., Fewell, R. R., & Meyer, D. J. (1986). Grandparents of children with special needs: Insights into their experiences and concerns. *Journal of the Division for Early Childhood, 10,* 36–44.

Valdés, G. (1996). *Con respeto: Bridging the distances between culturally diverse families and schools.* New York: Teachers College Press.

van Dijk, W. W., & Zeelenberg, M. (2002). What do we talk about when we talk about disappointment? Distinguishing outcome-related disappointment from person-related disappointment. *Cognition and Emotion, 16,* 787–807.

Walker-Dalhouse, D., & Dalhouse, A. D. (2001). Parent-school relations: Communicating more effectively with African American parents. *Young Children, 56*(4), 75–80.

Wang, M. C., Haertel, G. D., & Walberberg, H. J. (1993/1994). What helps students learn? *Educational Leadership, 52*(4), 74–79.

Wehman, P. (1990). School to work: Elements of successful programs. *TEACHING Exceptional Children, 23,* 40–43.

Williams, D. L., & Chavkin, N. (1989). Essential element of strong parent involvement programs. *Educational Leadership, 47*(2), 18–20.

Wolff, T. (2001). A practitioner's guide to successful coalitions. *American Journal of Community Psychology, 29,* 173–191.

Wright, J. W. (2001). *The New York Times Almanac: 2002.* New York: *New York Times.*

Wright, P. W. D., & Wright, P. D. (2001). *Wrightslaw: From emotions to advocacy—The special education survival guide.* Hartfield, VA: Harbor House Law Press.

Ysseldyke, J. E., Thurlow, M. L., Kozleski, E., & Reschly, D. (1998). *Accountability for the results of educating students with disabilities: Assessment conference report on the new assessment provisions of the 1997 amendments to the Individuals with Disabilities Act.* Minneapolis: University of Minnesota, National Center on Educational Outcomes.

Zellman, G. L., & Bell, R. M. (1990). *The role of professional background, case characteristics, and protective agency response in mandated child abuse reporting.* R-3825-HHS. Washington, DC: U.S. Department of Health and Human Services.

Zirkel, P. A. (1994). Overdue process revision for the Individuals with Disabilities Education Act. *Montana Law Review, 42.*

Index

Aaroe, L., 86
Abbott, C. F., 43, 44
Abrams, E. Z., 43
ACT testing accommodations, resource
    for, 156–157
Adolescent
    nonparticipation of parents of, 67–68
    sample letter to parents of, 144
    transition program and, 74–75
Advocate, working with, 59–60
Aggression, definition of, 17
Ainbinder, J. G., 134
Allen, Mary Ellen, 92, 96
Allen, N., 92, 119, 130
Alliances, with parents. *See* Parent–teacher
    relationship
Alper, S., 90
Altchech, M., 118, 124–125
Amador, N. A., 68, 131
Amani, Leslie, 59
Ambady, N., 6, 8
American Association of
    Retired Persons, 101
American Psychiatric Association, 22
Anderson, E., 68
Anderson, M. G., 85
Andrade, R., 131
Anger
    conflict stage of, 16–17
    cultural differences in, 19–20
    definition of, 17
    understanding, 17–19
    See also Angry parents
Angry parents, dealing with
    actions to avoid, 28
    always angry parents, 21
    dealing with own anger, 28–30

main principles for, 24 (tab)
    agree, 25
    be kind, 25–26
    be specific, 24–25
    remain calm, 24
narcissistic parents, 21–22
openly angry parents, 20–21
other strategies for
    active listening, 27
    clarify parents desired outcome,
        27–28
    reinforce positives, 26–27
safety concerns, 22–24
safety tips, 23 (tab)
self-reflection for, 31
summary of, 31
turning anger into action, 30–31
Artiles, A. J., 85
Asmus, J., 72

Back-to-School letter, 120
    sample, 146–148
Bailey, D. B., 49
Baker, M., 106
Baranowski, M. D., 103
Barrett-Kruse, C., 113
Barry, E., 66
Batson, C. D., 5
Bauch, P. A., 66
Baumeister, R. F., 22
Bean, G., 107
Bell, R. M., 110
Bellah, C. G., 30
Benson, H. A., 116
Berg, W., 72
Berkeley, T. R., 104, 105
Berla, N., 12

Bernard, S., 54, 115
Beutler, L. E., 78
Bhat, P., 51, 52, 54, 56, 58
Bickley, P. G., 68
Bielick, S., 48, 49
Bilhingsley, B. S., 36, 51, 84–85, 87, 91, 92
Blacher, J., 6, 39
Blanchard, L. W., 134
Bordin, J., 55, 121, 124, 128
Bost, P., 10
Boulware, B., 71
Boutte, G. S., 26
Brady, B. A., 86
Broughman, S. P., 48, 49
Brown, D., 101, 104
Brown, S. I., 5
Bryan, T., 26
Bryden, M. P., 19
Buehler, C., 106, 107
Bulman-Fleming, M. B., 19
Bursuck, W. D., 123, 124, 131
Bushman, B. J., 22

Campbell, M., 116
Campbell, S. B., 106
Campbell, W. K., 22
Caplan, G., 116
Caplan, R. B., 116
Carll, N., 113
Carnine, D., 49
Cavaiuolo, D., 90
Chandler, K., 48, 49
Chaumeton, N., 6, 8
Chavira, V., 39
Chavkin, N., 136
Child abuse/neglect, 110–113
Children and Adults with Attention
    Deficit Disorder, 42–43
Chinn, P. C., 85
Chrispeels, J. H., 65
Cialdini, R. B., 5
Citizen consumers, parents as, 50
Civil, M., 131
Clayton, E. W., 10
Cloutier, R., 68
Cohen, R., 59
Collaborative relationship. *See*
    Parent–teacher collaborative
    relationship
Collet-Klingenberg, L. L., 89
Comer, James, 71
Communication log, 10
    sample, 142
Conderman, G., 119

Connolly, K., 106
Connors, L. J., 68
Consortium to Evaluate Parent to
    Parent, 134
Consultant, responsibility of, 149–150
Coots, J. J., 51
Correa, V., 49
Council for Exceptional Children, 85
Cox, C. B., 101, 102
Culturally/linguistically diverse parents
    academic expectations for child, 51
    anger and, 19–20
    collaborative relationship with, 118–120
    lack of awareness of rights, 52
    noninvolvement *vs.* nonparticipation by,
        64–65
    nonparticipation by, 65, 69, 70
    overrepresentation in special education
        and, 85–86
    parent–teacher conference and, 124,
        125–126
    transition planning and, 75, 89–90
    view of child problems, 39
    view of disabilities, 119
Cutler, B. C., 50, 53, 84, 117, 137

Dalhouse, A. D., 127, 128
Danesco, E. R., 67
Dannison, L. L., 101, 102
Darling, N., 68
Darling, R. B., 34, 42, 102
Dauber, S. L., 118, 131, 137
Davies, D., 65
Day, M., 52
DeBettencourt, L. U., 18, 19
Defensiveness, difference from denial,
    36–38
Dekel, G., 6
Delgado-Gaitan, C., 65, 131
Dell, D. L., 86
Dell'Oliver, C., 116
Delpit, L. D., 52
Demertzis, A., 20
Denby, R., 107
Denial, by parents
    actions to avoid when dealing with, 44
    fostering hope in parents, 45
    harmful/not harmful, 39–40
    main principles for dealing with,
        41 (tab)
        ask why, 41–42
        encourage/exhort, 42–43
        wait, 40–41
    other strategies for dealing with, 43–44

self-reflection for, 45–46
summary of, 46
understanding, 34–36
vs. defensiveness, 36–38
vs. differences of opinion, 38–39
DeRaad, A., 72
Derby, K. M., 72
Deslandes, R., 68
DeSteno, N., 131
DeToledo, S., 101, 104
Detterman, D. K., 47
Diamond, K. E., 127
Dinnebeil, L. A., 121, 122
Dissatisfied parents
    actions to avoid when working with,
        60–61
    coping with consequences of working
        with, 53–55
    handling mediation/due process
        hearing, 55–56
    helping parents go beyond
        dissatisfaction, 61
    main principles for dealing with,
        56 (tab)
        ask for parents solution, 57–58
        focus on end goal, 58
        focus on problem/not person,
            56–57
    other strategies for dealing with,
        58–59
    recognizing context of dissatisfaction,
        48–50
    responding when parents reject IEP,
        52–53
    self-reflection for, 62
    summary of, 62
    understanding dissatisfaction, 50–52
    working with advocates, 59–60
Dodd, A. W., 58
Dombusch, S. M., 68
Dowdell, E. B., 101
Downing, J., 43
Downing, S., 43
Drugs/alcohol, parents under influence
    of, 23–24
Due process hearing/mediation, 55–56
Dull, V. T., 10

Edwards, A., 66
Emanuel, E. J., 76, 90
Enright, R., 30
Entman, S. S., 10
Epstein, J. L., 12, 64, 68, 117,
    118, 131, 137

Epstein, M. H., 123, 124, 131
Evans, C. B., 86, 103

Falbo, T., 68, 131
Family Educational Rights and Privacy
    Act (FERPA), 10
Federspiel, C. F., 10
Fewell, R. R., 103
Fielding, P. S., 55
Fields, T., 110
Fischer, A. H., 20
Fisher, R., 56, 93, 94
Fisher, Roger, 93
Fishman, N., 5
Fitzgerald, L. M., 123
Flett, A., 119
Florence County School District Four v.
    Carter, 49
Follmer, R., 12
Ford, M. S., 12
Forgas, J. P., 29
Forgive for Good (Luskin), 30
Forgiveness is a Choice (Luskin), 30
Forman, T. A., 117, 125, 136, 137
Forsyth, D. R., 17, 91, 95, 130
Foster parents, working with, 105–107
Frankel, R. M., 10
Friedman, B. B., 104, 105
From Emotions to Advocacy: The Special
    Education Survival Guide (Wright &
    Wright), 84

Garlington, J. A., 88
Gaudin, J. M., 106
Gauld-Jaeger, J., 10
Geenen, S., 69, 75
General education classroom teacher,
    responsibility of, 149
Githens, P. B., 10
Glanville, D., 20
Glass, J. C. Jr., 100, 101
Gold, S., 43, 44
Gollnick, D. M., 85
Göncü, A., 123
González, N., 131
Goodman, J. F., 43
Gorman, J. C., 51, 65
Grandparents, raising grandchildren
    as de facto parents, 103–104
    as secondary caregiver, 102–103
    custodial, 100–102
    resources for, 157
Granzin, A., 49
Green, S. E., 102

Greene, J., 9, 11
Greenfield, P. M., 118, 124–125
Griffin, C. C., 51, 52, 54, 56, 58
Grolnick, W. S., 131
Gross, J., 51
Group development, stages of, 16–17
Gut, D., 49

Haertel, G. D., 68
Hale, L. M., 121, 122
Hancock, R., 2, 64
Hand, B. M., 131
Harden, G. D., 39
Harden, T., 128, 129
Harding, J., 72
Harris, Y. R., 86
Harry, B., 39, 52, 69, 72, 78, 85, 90, 92, 118, 119, 123, 130
Hartshome, T., 10, 104
Hartwig, L. J., 34, 35
Harvard Negotiation Project, 93
Harvey, O. J., 95
Hastings, R. P., 103
Hayes, K. G., 87, 119
Henderson, A. T., 12
Hewison, J., 12, 64
Hickson, G. B., 10
Hill, R., 103
Hoerr, T. R., 126
Hogan, J., 55, 56
Home behavior log, 43, 72
Homeless families, working with, 107–110
Homer, R. H., 72
Homeschooling, 48–49
Homework, 130–132
Hood, W. R., 95
Hoover-Dempsey, K., 118, 131
Horwitz, S. M., 106
Hudson, P. J., 49, 73–74, 136
Hughes, M. T., 131
Huneycutt, T. L., 100, 101
Hunt, H., 107
Hurt, J. A., 99, 117, 136
Hutchins, M., 90

Ickes, W., 5
IDEA. *See* Individuals With Disabilities Act
IEP. *See* Individual Educational Program
In-group/out-group bias, 91
Individual Education Program (IEP), 5
    conducting meeting for, 128–130
    parental dissatisfaction and, 49, 54, 56

parental participation in, 72, 73–74
parental rejection of, 52–53
Individual transition plan (ITP), 72, 75, 89–91, 130
Individuals with Disabilities Education Act (IDEA), 2, 19, 49, 50, 55, 90, 123
Intake conference, 126
    sample letter for, 152
Interactive homework, 131
International Dyslexia Association, 43
ITP. *See* individual transition plan

Jacob, J., 70, 76
Jacob, S., 10, 104
Jargon, avoiding, 8, 92
Jaska, P., 132
Jayanthi, M., 123, 124, 131
Jayne, D., 90
Jensen, M. A., 16
Johnson, D. R., 76, 90
Johnson, J. L., 30
Jones, R., 64, 71, 73, 74, 86
Jones, S. S., 48
Jordan, L., 118, 119, 127
Josselson, R., 5

Kalyanpur, M., 52, 67, 88, 90, 123
Kauffman, Deborah, 132–133
Kaufman, H. O., 73–74
Keepler, D. L., 26
Keith, P. B., 68
Keith, T. Z., 68
Kerem, E., 5
Kilpatrick, S. D., 30
Kirschenbaum, H., 136, 137
Kishinevsky, Vera, 63, 77, 78, 83, 95–96
Kosmoski, C. J., 23, 27, 28
Kozleski, E., 49
Kratochwill, T. R., 118
Krikston, D., 106
Kübler-Ross, E., 34, 45

Laffey, P., 72
Lake, J. F., 36, 51, 84–85, 87, 91, 92
Lamborn, S. D., 68
LaMorte, M. W., 10
Lane, H. B., 118, 119, 127
Laplante, D., 6, 8
Lardieri, L. A., 6
Learning disabilities, resources for, 155–156
LeClerc, D., 68
Lee, S., 68

Lee, Y., 119
Lein, L., 68, 131
Leon, E., 69
Lerner, J., 40
Letter to parents (sample)
    Back-to-School letter, 146–148
    intake conference letter, 152
    of adolescent, 144
    of older elementary student, 143
    welcome letter, 141
Levinson, W., 6, 8, 10
Lewis, A. E., 117, 125, 136, 137
Lewis, B., 5
Leyser, Y., 6
Litz, K. K., 12
Lopez, N., 65
Lopez, S. R., 39
Lopez-Vasquez, A., 69, 75
Lovitt, T. C., 49, 75, 76
Low SES parents, educational expectations
    for children, 51–52, 65
Luce, C., 5
Luecking, R., 76, 90
Luskin, F., 30
Lytle, R. K., 55, 121, 124, 128

Mack, M., 76, 90
Maiers, A., 124
Mandal, M., 19
Manning, D., 44
Manstead, A. S. R., 20
Marquis, J. G., 134
Marschall, M., 50, 52
Martin, R., 17
Martinez, E., 113
Mathur, S., 26
Matier, P., 48
Matlosz, F. C., 49
Matsumoto, D., 19
Maxwell, K. L., 137
May, M., 48
McCullough, M. E., 29, 30, 106
McDonald, L., 42, 45
McDowell, S. A., 48
McEwan, E. K., 6, 17, 18, 19, 27, 28, 66
McLaughlin, M., 92, 119, 130
McMahan, G. A., 78
McNair, J., 74
McNeal, R. B., 68, 69
McWilliam, R. A., 137
Mediation/due process hearing,
    55–56
Menlove, R. R., 49, 73–74, 136

Meyer, D. J., 103
Miller, C. S., 10
Minority overrepresentation, in special
    education, 85–87
Mistrust, by parents
    actions to avoid when dealing with, 96
    during transition planning, 89–91
    main principles for dealing with,
        94 (tab)
        acknowledge mistrust openly, 93–94
        find common ground, 94–95
        make amends, 94
    other strategies for dealing with, 95–96
    preventing, 91–93
    reason for
        bureaucracy/hierarchy of education
            system, 87
        discomfort with/dislike of school, 89
        negative experience with school, 88
        overrepresentation of minority, 85–87
        school financial concerns, 87
        teacher snap judgment of child, 87–88
        unfair blame for child problem, 88
    self-reflection for, 97
    summary of, 97–98
    taking parents beyond, 97
Mitrani, Judith, 1
Modell, S. J., 91
Moliero, C., 78
Moll, L., 131
Morningstar, M. E., 74, 75, 76
Morris, Kristi, 126, 127
Mosley-Howard, G. S., 86, 103
Mourning, stages of, 34, 45
Muller, C., 68
Mullooly, J. P., 10
Munk, D. D., 123, 124, 131

Narcissistic parents, dealing with, 21–22
NAS. *See* National Academy of Sciences
National Academy of Sciences (NAS), 51
National Center on Child Abuse and
    Neglect, 110
National Clearinghouse for Professions in
    Special Education, 85
Nelson, J., 86, 123, 124, 131
Neuberg, S. L., 5
Nguyen, T., 6, 8
Nistler, R. J., 124
No Child Left Behind Act, 48
Noncustodial parents, working with,
    104–105
Nonparticipation/resistance, by parents

actions to avoid when dealing with, 79–80
culturally/linguistically diverse parents, 64–65, 69, 70
helping parents go beyond, 80
main principle for eliciting participation, 70 (tab)
  be creative, 71
  confront resistance, 72–73
  get to know parents, 69–70
  help parents participate, 73–74
  increase participation in transition planning, 74–76
other strategies for dealing with, 76–79
self-reflection for, 80
summary of, 81
understanding nonparticipation, 66–67
of parents of adolescent, 67–68
vs. noninvolvement, 64–65
Nontraditional family, working with
  family of suspected child abuse/neglect, 110–113
  foster parents, 105–107
  grandparents
    as de facto parents, 103–104
    as secondary caregiver, 102–103
    custodial, 100–102
  homeless families, 107–110
  main points for, 106 (tab)
  noncustodial parents, 104–105
  self-reflection for, 113–114
  summary of, 114
Nowicki, S. Jr., 20
Nunnelley, J. C., 110

Okagaki, L., 127
Okun, B. F., 6, 7
Olson Bermudez, Laura, 33, 35, 41
Orme, J. G., 106, 107
Outcome-related disappointment, 61

Parent mentor, 134–135
Parent–teacher collaborative relationship
  cultural considerations in, 118–120
  end-of-year concerns
    getting/giving feedback, 134
    recruiting parent mentor, 134–135
  family-friendly school role in, 136–137
  initiating
    by building credibility, 120–121
    by defining roles, 123
    by motivating parents, 122–123
    by using interpersonal skills, 121–122

main points for, 135 (tab)
maintaining
  by conducting IEP/ITP/large group meeting, 128–130
  by dealing with homework, 130–132
  by establishing boundaries/support system, 132–134
  by handling conflict, 130
  by holding parent–teacher conference, 124–128
realistic expectations for, 137–138
resolving reservations about, 116–118
self-reflection for, 138
stages of, 116
summary of, 139
See also Parent–teacher relationship
Parent–teacher conference, 124–128
  sample summary sheet for, 153
Parent–teacher relationship
  avoiding lawsuit, 9–12
  benefits of, 2, 12
  developing alliance, 3–5
  effective communication and, 6–7
  effective communication skills for, 8 (tab)
  giving/receiving feedback, 4–5
  obstacle to gaining cooperation, 2–3
  poor communication and, 7–9
  poor communication skills for, 9 (tab)
  role of empathy in, 5–6
  self-reflection for, 12–13
  summary of, 13
  See also Parent–teacher collaborative relationship
Parental involvement/participation
  benefit of, 12
  equity/advocacy in, 123
  sample letter to parents about benefit of, 143, 144
  teacher view on, 64
  See also Nonparticipation/resistance, by parents
Parents, responsibility of, 150
Parents Anonymous, 113
A Parent's Guide to Innovative Education (Dodd), 58
Parent observation sheet, 145
Parette, P., 78
Patton, B., 56, 93, 94
Patton, J. M., 85, 86
Peck Peterson, S. M., 72
Peel, B. B., 118, 119, 127
Peel, H. A., 118, 119, 127
Peplau, L. A., 17, 18

Person-related disappointment, 61
Pichert, J., 10
Pollack, D. R., 23, 27, 28
Polloway, E. A., 123, 124, 131
Potvin, P., 68
Powers, L. E., 69, 75
Powers, L. K., 134
Prehearing conference (PHC), 55
Preston, Jeana, 64
*The Principle's Quick-Reference Guide to
    School Law* (Dunklee & Shoop), 12
Prouty, A., 72

Quiroz, B., 118, 124–125

Racism, 86
Ramirez, F., 120
Rao, S., 67, 88, 111, 119
Rapport, M. J. K., 51, 52, 54, 56, 58
Reform, education, 48
Renzaglia, A., 90
Reschly, D., 49
Resource-room teacher, responsibility of,
    149–150
Resources
    for ACT testing accommodations,
        156–157
    for attention deficit/hyperactivity
        disorder, 42–43, 155
    for grandparents raising
        grandchildren, 157
    for learning disabilities, 43, 155–156
    for other disabilities, 156
    general, on special education, 154–155
Reyes-Blanes, M. E., 118, 119, 127
Ribas, W. B., 120
Rindfleisch, N., 107
Rivero, E., 65
Roch, C., 50, 52
Rodriguez, J. A., 49, 75, 76
Rodriguez, P., 49
Rodriguez-Mosquera, P. M., 20
Rosenthal, R., 6, 8
Ross, A., 48
Roter, D. L., 10
Rothenberg, D., 101
Royer, E., 68
Rueda, R., 90
Rule, S., 121, 122
Rusch, E. R., 74

Sagarin, B. J., 5
Sanchez, A. R., 48

Sandler, H., 118, 131
Santelli, B., 116, 134
Sarason, S. B., 137
Schilmoeller, G. L., 103
Schindler, P. J., 44
Schloss, P. J., 90
Schneider, B., 119
Schneider, M., 50, 52
School administrator, responsibility of,
    150–151
School choice, 48
School psychologist, responsibility of, 150
Schumm, J. S., 131
Scorgie, K., 42, 45
Sears, D. O., 17, 18
Section 504, of Rehabilitation Act of 1973,
    18–19, 122
Seligman, M., 34, 42, 102
Serpell, R., 123
Shapiro, J., 39
Shaw, L. L., 5
Sheridan, S. M., 118
Sherif, C. W., 95
Sherif, M., 95
Shymansky, J. A., 131
Siegel-Causey, E., 116
Simms, M. D., 106
Simon, R., 106
Singer, G. H. S., 134
Singh, K., 68
Siu, S-F., 51, 65, 125
Skinner, D., 49
Skrtic, T., 123
Sloan, F. A., 10
Sloper, K. M., 137
Slowiaczek, M. L., 131
Smith, A. B., 101, 102
Smith, T. E. C., 55
Special education, resources for,
    154–155
Spindler, G., 86
Spindler, L., 86
Sporer, S. L., 22
Steere, D. E., 90
Steinberg, L., 68
Stodden, R. A., 76, 90
Stoner, E. A., 72
Stowitschek, J. J., 49, 75, 76
Stucke, T. S., 22
Student Study Team, 128
Sullivan, K., 26
Sullivan, M. E., 134
Summers, J. A., 116

Suter, D., 49, 73–74, 136
Sutphen, R., 106
Swanson, H. L., 6
Swick, K. J., 107–109
Swing-shifter, 3

Talbert-Johnson, C., 86
Talebi, H., 78
Tao, L., 71
Taylor, S. E., 17, 18
Teachers Involve Parents in Schoolwork
    (TIPS), 131
*Teachers Involve Parents in Schoolwork
    (TIPS) Interactive Homework Training
    Materials* (Epstein & Van Voorhis), 131
Team member, responsibility of
    consultant/resource-room teacher,
        149–150
    general education classroom
        teacher, 149
    parents, 150
    school administrator, 150–151
    school psychologist, 150
Terry, B. Z., 26
Teske, P., 50, 52
Thompson, L. A., 47
Thurlow, M. L., 49
TIPS (Teachers Involve Parents in
    Schoolwork), 131
Tolfo, Richard, 35
Törestad, B., 17
Trainor, A., 90
Trent, S. C., 85
Tribble, I., 86
Tripp, Lynda, 105
Trivette, P., 68
Trueba, H., 65
Trust
    recognizing value of, 84–85
    See also Mistrust, by parents
Trusty, J., 68
Tucker, C. M., 86
Tuckman, B. W., 16
Turnbull, A. P., 50, 74, 75, 76, 116
Turnbull, H. R., 50, 74, 75, 76
Tyler, V. S., 26

U.S. Census Bureau, 101
U.S. General Accounting Office, 55

Ulrich, S., 72
Unterberg, Adele, 55
Ury, W., 56, 57, 93, 94

Vach-Hasse, T., 101, 102
Vadasy, P. F., 103
Valdés, G., 69
Valdez, L., 91
Van Dijk, W. W., 61
Van Voorhis, F. L., 131
Vaughn, S., 131
Volunteer, classroom, 3, 4–5
Volunteer communication notebook, 5

Wacker, D. P., 72
Walberberg, H. J., 68
Walker-Dalhouse, D., 127, 128
Wan, C. K., 17
Wang, M. C., 68
Warin, J., 66
Watson, D., 17
Wehman, P., 2
Weithorn, L., 106
Welcome letter, for parents (sample), 141
West, S., 107
Whetten-Goldstein, K., 10
White, B. J., 95
Wilgosh, L., 42, 45
Williams, D. L., 136
Wolff, T., 122
Worthington, E. L. Jr., 30
Wosencroft, Donna-Jean, 15, 26
Wright, J. W., 91
Wright, P. D., 84
Wright, P. W. D., 84

Yore, L. D., 131
*You, Your Child and Special Education: A
    Guide to Making the System Work*
    (Cutler), 84
Ysseldyke, J. E., 49

Zeelenberg, M., 61
Zellman, G. L., 110
Zirkel, P. A., 55